THE ENDLESS ROAD
STRUGGLES TO STRENGTH

MABLE GREEN

Order this book online at www.trafford.com
or email orders@trafford.com

Most Trafford titles are also available at major online book retailers.

Printed in the United States of America.

ISBN: 978-1-4669-8775-3 (sc)
ISBN: 978-1-4669-8777-7 (hc)
ISBN: 978-1-4669-8776-0 (e)

Library of Congress Control Number: 2013905889

Trafford rev. 11/07/2013

 www.trafford.com

North America & international
toll-free: 1 888 232 4444 (USA & Canada)
fax: 812 355 4082

CONTENTS

Acknowledgements

MANY HAVE INFLUENCED AND contributed to the contents of this book. Your help went far beyond what I'd hoped for. I especially value your love, respect, kindness, and consideration.

To my grandparents who gave me hope, to my parents who gave me love, inspiration, and wisdom, to my husband and children who gave me love, support, and encouragement, to my brothers, sisters, and cousins, who shared their love, interest, and support, to my nieces and nephews for their love, respect, and dedication.

To Scarlett Sips, Honorable Mayor Willie Earl Spencer, Barbara Robinson, Linda Ervin, Janette Tigner, Louise Manhein, Donna Hawks, Dr. Rick J. Carlisle, Beth Hanna, Thomas Polk, Michael Miller, Bethany Miller, Roy Walker, Arness Bowden, Paula Wilhite, Jillian Wisely, Cynthia Scott, Bobby Doyle for their respect and support.

To Carlos De-Richard Woods, illustrated the school for his support

To my dear coworker and friend, Stephanie Turner, illustrated the tree for her support

To Trafford Publishing staff members for their guidance and support throughout the publishing process.

INTRODUCTION

E VERYONE CAN READ THIS book simply because it can inspire you. It can be shared not only with family members but friends and readers alike. It includes pictures and history. This information can link you to poems of dedication, inspirational and personal stories, with fond memories, that will touch a soft spot in your heart and, along the way, enjoy some laughter.

You can feel and see the struggles, doubts, fears, and tears a time of trying to hold on and finally letting go, learning that, sometimes, when you regret leaving one type of living or struggle, you can live a little better someplace else and somehow. But there were plenty of prayers, love, and hope. They found strength to move forward. And here we are sharing their stories of their strengths.

As you might have heard, the mind is like an umbrella or parachute. It works best when it is open. There are memories and storytelling of our deceased. I hope you will enjoy. Readers may be able to follow and connect with my stories.

It is based on love, survival, patience, losses, understanding and some of my life experiences.

The Endless Road: Struggles to Strength is a must read for all ages. There are related stories that some readers may have already experienced. The contents can expand your vision on some past history and the present. You can travel with the author from the 1800s from the hardship of slavery to a land of better opportunities. You can continue to travel on an inspirational journey with our daily reading and good rules.

DOES GOD CARE?

D OES GOD MAKE A way and answer prayers? Wesley B. Weaver would answer a resounding yes in these encouraging and funny stories after so many hard days shared on the farm with her parents, sisters and brothers, and husband and family. One could not help but to have prayer in their life.

This country woman from the hills of Tennessee was wise and very encouraging to others. Struggle after struggle, she stayed focus on raising her children with her husband.

They drew strength from one another and determined to make it on a daily basis. Even though life was hard they continued to make the best of it. They weren't quitters by any means.

No matter how little they had, it was always just enough to share their blessings with someone else. The neighbors and friends in the town of Bolivar returned the favor. The word respect was very much honored by our parents. And we were taught this every day. This is what made this small town special.

The children played together. They shared with each other as well. They made up their own games and had plenty of fun doing it. This was a place where violence was rare doing this period of the 60s and 70s.

However, racism did exist. Some wanted to date but could not. There were opposite race that were family members and could not discuss it.

All in all, this was a peaceful, fun, loving, and praying place to live. There were plenty of animals in the woods to be killed for food. There were vegetable gardens and fruit trees. Apple, peach, blackberry, and plum pies were something to enjoy. The livestock provided transportation, food, and helped with labor. Yes, it was a time that we wanted much more and that more eventually came.

HISTORY

I T ALL BEGAN ON a farm about ten miles from Bolivar, Tennessee in Hardeman County. It was a place with many unanswered questions. As a young person, when you grew up in the country and lived about a mile from a main highway and six miles from the nearest town, you felt out of touch without any civilization. Your freedom was limited due to your parenting, location, and transportation.

We lived on about thirty acres of land that my grandfather owned. It was and is a beautiful place to enjoy. I can say that now that I am an adult. When I look back, I can appreciate the natural beauty and the quietness of nature and the privacy. When I was a child, these things did not appeal to me as much; if at all.

My parents were born and raised in Bolivar, Tennessee, in Hardeman County. My mother Wesley B. lived on a farm with the guidance of her mother, Ollie and father, John Wesley. She had four sisters and four brothers who shared the living quarters with her. She learned how to raise her own food and store the food for the winter months. She was capable of making clothes and killing wild game. My dad was raised by his mother, Anna and dad, Marion. He learned at an early age how to work hard and survive and provide for a family.

My mom was around fifteen years old when she met my dad. This was conveyed to me by my older siblings. Daddy showed up on a horse with his long legs hanging from the sides of the horse. My mom was in the garden with her sisters at the time. They courted for a while. Then one day, my dad asked for her hand in marriage.

They got married, hitched, or jumped the broom so to speak. It was my understanding that dad's Uncle Nolan married them on December 26, 1926. My mom had just turned 16 and dad was 19 years old. I look back at the ages of my mother and my great grandparents. I think about how today society stress concerns about under age marriages.

After my mother married my dad, my grandmother Anna gave momma a pair of old overalls filled with holes to patch. They were the worst pair of overalls he had. This was for Grandma Anna to test momma's sewing skills. My mom said she patch those overalls to a tee. She made an impression on her ability to sew.

In this union thirteen children were born with possibly one miscarriage along the way. All thirteen children did not live in the house at the same time. As the elder brothers and sisters moved on more children were added to the family.

The town of Bolivar and the Hardeman County area is a remarkable place to live. It holds some interesting history. I've learned that Hardeman County originated around 1823 from the Hardin County and Indian land. As far as the history of Bolivar I learned that Bolivar was originally named Hatchie Town. It sits on the bank of the Hatchie River. The name was later changed to Bolivar to honor Simon Bolivar the Liberator of Colombia and Venezuela. The town began as a trading post. The Chickasaw tribe gathered to trade with the first settlers in the area. The town was union-occupied pretty much throughout the civil war. In the historic districts featured are antebellum homes and other structures. Antebellum mean historical, colonial, or early eighteenth and nineteenth century. Bolivar holds a quite of bit of history. It remains to be a quiet and friendly town.

This is The Little Courthouse. History is reserved here from the 1800s. This little courthouse was built in 1824. It was the first log courthouse and jail for the Hardeman County area. You will learn as well as I have that there were famous people that visited the Hardeman County area like President James K. Polk, Davy Crockett, and Thomas Edison.

In the center of Bolivar across from the old Bolivar Bank sits the court house. This court house dates back to 1868. On the grounds you will be able to view a monument to the civil war soldiers that came from Hardeman County. A bust of Simon Bolivar is located in front of the Hardeman County Court House. It was a gift from the people of Venezuela. This courthouse sat across the street from the bank.

Bolivar Court House

Bust of Simon Bolivar

There was a clothing store that sat on the same street as the Ben Franklin five-and-dime store. The Five and Dime store sat northwest of the court house across the street. It was known more in small towns. It was named after Benjamin Franklin. It was mentioned that it was around 1927 when established. Many years later filed bankruptcy.

Bolivar Hardeman County Library

Southeast across the street from the courthouse is the Bolivar Public Library. I found out that the library was first organized and sponsored by the Tuesday Club in 1954 where a lady name Lillian Bills began the first circulation of books. It was indeed a great thing for this community. As the area grew so did the books in the library. This increased knowledge and education for the Hardeman County and the surrounding areas.

When I was growing up in the Hardeman County area, I never used the Library in Bolivar nor Middleton. The only Library I had access to be inside the schools of Bolivar Industrial and Middleton High School. The school library in both schools served the purpose for my class work. However, my knowledge could have been extended maybe if I had used the public Library. Taking care of farm business was what was most important to our parents at the time.

Bolivar Bank

The old bank was in business in 1886. In 1914, the bank built one of the most modern bank buildings in West Tennessee located in Bolivar. This was the bank that my dad and mom did their business. It caught a fire a few years ago. It is not open for business. In 1981, the bank built the present building CB & S Bank.

Down on the east end of town, there was a place call the T-Room. This was where the teens hung out, smoked cigarettes, and played pool. There were many teens that were not allowed inside the place simply because of the smoking and pool playing. There were several residents that had family that were very strict. Church was a very big part of growing up in this community. There were rules and rules had to be followed.

I recall a minister that had a daughter that kind of wandered herself up to the T-Room one night. Her curiosity got the best of her. The dad found out about it. He kindly went to the place and escorted her out. If you think you were going to bring shame to the church going people, you had another thing coming. When rules were made, you followed them. It was best to follow the rules before bringing embarrassment to yourself or your family. A lesson learned.

This was known as Sun Rise Inn

Just a few feet below were a café. It was called Sun Rise Inn. It was run by Ms. Cleo Williams. This was where sandwiches, ice cream, and pops were sold. Inside there were booths with a jukebox and a counter with stools. In the back was a pool room. And a big office sat to the left. This was where the insurance office of Mr. Ned Rawls was located.

Next door upstairs was a hotel for overnight stay for people from out of town. I do not think teenagers were allowed. Plus no one had the money to spend. And everyone in town would have known the exact time you checked in and checked out. You could also look it up in the newspaper. Next to this hotel was a room that opened up for the teens to dance. All this room had was a jukebox and a couple of chairs.

Next to this room was a small store front market that used to set on the corner. We had markets there in town when I grew up. I recall some of them as being, Creek-more, Maxwell and Piggly Wiggly Markets.

When I was growing up Bolivar did not have a hospital. Later Bolivar General was built around the early 70s. It is an affiliate of West Tennessee Healthcare. They are serving the Hardeman County and the surrounding communities.

Lorenza Miller   John Archie Williams   Ned Rawls   Jorome Boyd   Michael Miller

On the west of town is the Dixie Funeral Home. The only funeral home for African American's at the time I grew up was this funeral home. This facility set on the west of the town. It has been in business since 1946. Mr. Lorenzo Miller and Mr. Ned Rawls saw a great opportunity to purchase the funeral home. After the purchasing the establishment, they hired Mr. Joe Boyd, Mr. John Archie Williams, and Mr. Roy Buntyn. Years later joining their staff were Mr. Willie Turner and Mr. Ben Murrell. The funeral home is located on Bills Street in Bolivar. Mr. Lorenzo Miller was also our high school principal and a notary. Mr. Jerome Boyd was also a notary and the mortician. This group of people served the community well with compassion for the people. It is being run now by Mr. Michael Miller, JD. He is the funeral director and embalmer. He and his family are also serving the community with compassion for the people.

In this near area of town was an Ice Plant. On holiday's my parents purchased a block of ice and put in the top of our old refrigerator. At the time we did not have electricity. I can remember chipping away at the block of ice with the ice pick.

Also on the west end of town was then known as Western State Hospital. It is known now as Western Mental Health Institute. The Institute serves around twenty five surrounding counties for long-term and forensic services for individuals. It is a respectable and well known place.

Down to the north end of town, there was a restaurant called the McNeal's Restaurant. It was located along the alley, just around the corner from the theater. There were two restrooms along the alley way. A few feet from there, Aunt Lil would barbecue and sell sandwiches. I think the cost was about thirty-five cents per sandwich.

We had a donut shop in the heart of town. I have always thought that they had the best fresh hot and soft donuts in the world. I could never make up my mind which one to purchase.

Luez Theatre

We had one movie theater in town. It was called the Luez Theater. At the time I was coming up, the African American people were only allowed to go upstairs in the balcony. The whites only sat downstairs on the first floor. As I think about it, we had the best seats. We could always see and not worry about anyone walking in front of the screen. Years later, everyone sat where they wanted to. It is my understanding that the Luez Theater was built in 1940. And it was run by a lady named Louise Mask. It was told that she did not tolerate giggling, talking, or sitting too close together. She walked the aisles and threatened to stop the movie and turned on the house lights if anyone stepped out of line. Unfortunately, the theater was recently closed in 2012.

In town many years ago there was a Bryant shoe store which is now closed. I can remember going into a shoe store sitting along the main street in town. One Saturday, Daddy gave me two dollars to purchase a pair of tennis shoes for my gym class. This was a Saturday to remember. I was afraid of the lady in the store. I just picked up a pair of white shoes and paid for them. She asked me if I wanted to try them on. I shook my head no and ran after paying for them. Mom was not with us at the time.

After getting home, I learned that the shoes were too small. I forced myself to wear them. I had to have the shoes on Monday for gym. It was too late to tell Daddy after getting them home. I guess this is why I have corns today.

Bolivar has grown now with several fast food places, hotels, and restaurants. Wal-Mart and many other stores have been added to this lovely community.

Bolivar Bulletin Times

One place that has been in business in Bolivar a long time is the newspaper. "Bolivar Bulletin Times" newspaper has been a dependable paper over the years. History has it that the first newspaper appeared in Bolivar was called Bolivar Palladium in 1829. Bolivar Bulletin was purchased in 1888. The paper will print anything from check bouncing, speeding tickets, and automobile accidents to going to jail. This includes all the latest news. This newspaper has been powerful in helping to keep the community up to date and safe. It is my understanding that in July 2013, the newspaper brought home a five press award for best news. This is proof of the good work the newspaper is doing.

Also, there is good work still existing in the areas with the cotton fields, hay fields, vegetable gardens, fruit trees, and other land that are being worked for the convenience of the community. The fresh fruits and vegetables are great. Several more churches have been built. The homes are beautiful to see. The quietness in the rural country side is still something to enjoy. The warm southern hospitality is wonderful. As you drive by people there still throw their hands up to wave even when they do not have any idea who you are.

When we were growing up, we thought that people had it better than us. And many did have it better. After school our bus driver had to stop and get gas. For some reason we would get all excited, especially the younger students. The drivers had the bus filled up because they were assigned to drive the bus at night when we had school programs.

Three Way-Grocery

There was a Three Way Grocery Store. It was built in 1945 according to Scarlett Sips. She purchased the store as of 2009. The students begged the bus driver to stop at this Grocery store to buy candy after school. Some students had a little money and some did not. Yet, the students looked forward to stopping at the store.

One place we did not look forward to was the cotton field. We raised our own cotton. We picked enough cotton to fill the trailer. Daddy took the cotton to the cotton gin. A cotton gin is a machine that quickly and easily separated the cotton from its seeds. The cotton fibers are processed into clothing or other cotton goods. The undamaged seeds were replanted or used for cottonseed oils.

The cotton gin machine was invented by Eli Whitney in (1793-1825).

We had two cotton gins in the area. We took the filled trailers of cotton to be weighed and filtered. It was located in Bolivar on the south end of town. Middleton cotton gin was located on the east side of town. Daddy prayed each time for the weight of the cotton to be enough so that he could have enough funds to take care of the family. It was fun riding on the back of the trailer on top of the cotton. It could be dangerous if not careful. The adults always looked out for the children as they drove. There were many times they told us to sit down.

The city of Bolivar has a city Mayor and a Hardeman County Mayor. According to the Mayor's office the first city mayor of Bolivar was the Honorable Alferd Coats in 1889. The first Hardeman County Mayor was Honorable William Ramsey in 1825.

The *Honorable* Mayor Barrett Stevens is the serving mayor of the city of Bolivar. Mayor Stevens has served over sixteen years as Councilman and mayor. He is a retired Army National Guard Command Sergeant major. Paula Wilhite is the Municipal Court Clerk.

The Honorable Mayor Willie Earl Spencer is the first African-American to serve as the Hardeman County Mayor. He is now serving his second term.

Things have changed quite a bit in Hardeman County. The community changed in some ways and so did the people. Yet there are still some memories of the old way of living from the 60s and 70s.

Middleton was considered to be a smaller town than Bolivar. The serving mayor of Middleton is The Honorable Jackie Cox. The town continues to grow. Middleton has convenient shopping. J.P. Shelly & Sons, Dollar General Store, Gift shops, Gas stations and Tire Services, Shackleford Funeral Home, Get Well & Dollar Store, Kirk's Supermarket, Fancy and Middleton Flower Shops, Henderson storage and Yopp's Storage, and Restaurants. There are Medical facility's serving the community.

Middleton Community Public Library

Middleton Community Library is located on Bolton Avenue in Middleton Tennessee. After a meeting was held in October 1974, it was then a decision was made to open the library. 1975 open house was held and the library was open for business. All are serving the community of Middleton and the surrounding areas. Ms. Kathy Carter is the director. She has been since 2005. Prior to 2013, the directors were Mrs. Pulliam, Helen Brint, Diana Hunter, Gayle Hobbs, Kathy Carter, and Wanza Taylor. The Middleton Library is still growing strong and serving the community to its fullest.

The area has several industrial manufactures located in the area and employs more than a thousand people in the community. I learned that the town was founded around 1849. It was chartered and was name Middleton in honor of Memphis and Charleston official.

Shackelford Funeral Home

The Shackelford Funeral Directors began operation in Savannah, Tennessee in October 1926. Robert Shackelford Sr. moved to Bolivar in 1932. The Funeral home is being serviced by dedicated family members. The main chapel is located in Bolivar Tennessee. There is also a location in Middleton, Tennessee.

Also servicing the Hardeman County areas is the Hardeman County Funeral Service located on South Porter Street in Bolivar. The owner of this establishment is Mr. Timothy M. Sanders. The serving director and manager is Mr. James L. Gray, Jr.

Bolivar Fire Department

The Bolivar and Middleton Fire Department are continuing to service the Hardeman County Community for a safe environment. Bolivar fire chief is Chief Lynn Price. The department is protecting around ten thousand residents in the Hardeman County area. Middleton Fire Chief is Chief Jerry Vaughn. The department protects around ten thousand residents. The Middleton Fire Department is a volunteer fire department with a "5" rating.

Many homes are so far away from the city limits. Servicing the country areas I'm sure has it challenges. I think back to years ago how the wooden frame homes burned pretty fast. Safety had to be a real issue for the residents.

Middleton Police Department (2012) in Middleton, Tennessee

Middleton police chief is David Lynn Webb. In 2004, Middleton police department hired Mr. Arness Bowden as their first African American to their team. He became the first African American to make sergeant. They hired patrolman, Mr. Gustavo Salto their first Hispanic-American to the force in 2006. Also, on the team is patrolman, Mr. Richie Webb. All are serving well in keeping the community safe.

As often as I have seen the police station in Bolivar and Middleton I have never paid too much attention to them. When I was growing up I did not hear about anyone I knew going to jail. Bolivar and Middleton Police department has grown and many changes have been made compared to the 60s and 70s.

Hardeman County Sheriff Department

Julius Caesar Nichols Robertson was elected the first Bolivar sheriff and tax collector in 1823. It is believed that he tried to retire but the people during that time would not let him. He died at the age of 87.

In speaking with Thomas Polk it is my understanding that Mr. John Archie Williams was the first serving African American assistant chief of police for the City of Bolivar Police Department. I can remember him being on the force when I was in school. The first African American city deputies were two brothers Joseph and Thomas Parham. Later, the first African American chief of police for the city of Bolivar was Mr. Bill Irons. Now serving as Police Chief of Bolivar is Chief James P. Bake.

Bolivar Police Department
(1824 first jail used-see The Little courthouse information)

The first African-American that served as county sheriff was Mr. Delphus Van Hicks. He served several years.

Mr. John Doolen now serves the community as the county sheriff.

While the family lived on the old place, I was too young to remember anything about it. I was told that I was around three years old when we moved from this home. The first seven sisters and brothers lived in this home before leaving the south. They all moved to Michigan for a better opportunity.

The old house was described and remembered best by my brother Carl and sister Allie.

The old house was called by this name because this was the old Weaver place. It was not painted. The front porch faced the east. When you walked into a big hallway on the southwest side, left of the hallway was where momma and daddy slept. That was called the master bedroom with a fireplace. The kitchen was north of that bedroom. The sleeping quarters for the children were off the hallway, as you walked in on the right.

The barn sat west of the house. The shed sat south of the house. The fruit orchard was close to the vegetable garden, which sat left of the house. Fields were at the back of the house.

Daddy and Momma rented the house and land from a lady by the name of Ms. Cruther's. The rent consisted of one 500 pounds of a bale of cotton, which equaled about $130.00. She ended up with the land after Grandma Anna and Grandpa Marion died.

When Momma and Daddy did not hear from her after a while, Momma got worried. She started writing letters with no return. They were thinking maybe the woman had become ill or possibly died. She lived in Knoxville, Tennessee. The only way Momma knew how to reach her was by letters only. She wrote more than once. Previously, she came down with her friend once a year to collect the rent and bragged on Momma's famous biscuits.

A man took over the land by paying the unpaid taxes. Daddy went to the court along with his brother. And when they went to court, they weren't allowed to speak as freely as they would have liked. Of course, they lost the case. Back during this time, it was well known that if you speak up for yourself, you would here, "Boy, don't you dispute my word." End of interview.

Time has changed. Some people have changed. Many opportunities have increased. Regardless whether they were unable to pay rent due to lack of money and the crops not growing or the place were up for sale they left one place and come to enjoy another. I often wonder why momma and daddy did not go into town and inquire about the land before things had gotten so bad for them. I do know there were a lot of things daddy did not know about. If rent was collected only once a year, a lot can happen with transactions during that time without you knowing. I guess this is why he and momma relied on my sister Clinora to take care of their business when she had gotten older. From the sound of things the move they made end up being better for the family. My parents struggled to pay the rent but a door of opportunity opened for them to put a roof over their family head.

Even though I do not remember moving from the old place to the new place, I can remember the conversations about how we struggled to make ends meet. The farming was a hard way of life to provide for your family. All the crops relied on was us working the land and the precious rain from god. There were times the crops did not do as well one year compared to maybe the prior year.

When we made this move and as time went on with fewer children in the household it made the load a little lighter for the family. We learned to be grateful for whatever you had. We also knew that other families had it hard as well.

With the older children moving to the north for better job opportunities, this was a blessing for the family they left. After getting jobs, they were able to send gifts and money home. Even though we moved, we still appreciated all the help we could receive.

Upon the move to the new house with my grandfather, it opened some doors for us. He had planted plenty of fruit trees on the property, which helped with food. The old place held memories for the older siblings that I did not have. I can't begin to imagine being forced out of your house and off the property you once lived on. It must have been heart breaking especially with a bunch of children.

Rev. John Wesley with grandson Carnell
August 1956 House built by Grandpa

We basically did not have any place to go. Momma talked to her dad known as my Grandpa West. And we moved on the new place with him. Grandpa was living in the house alone that he built. Columbus, West, Allie, Eunice, and Arthur had all moved to Detroit. James, Freddie, Clinora, Carl, Carnell, and Mable moved to the new house.

Thank god for Grandpa West. If it wasn't for him who knows where we would have been! My parents had six more children that had not left home. When we moved this made eight people move in on Grandpa. I can see why he courted Ms. Hattie married and moved out.

There was another house on the new place before we moved. Grandpa West and Grandma Ollie lived in it. This is where Grandma died. I did not remember when we first moved in the new place that my grandfather built. I was about 3 years old at the time. But, I lived there until I graduated high school. This was the home I remembered.

The new house story

This picture was taken from Aunt Lil's front yard after everyone had moved out, after the death of Momma and Daddy. This house has been demolished. One of my brothers has rebuilt and lives on the land. On the hill; you would see a house to the right. This is where Momma's sister, Lillie, lived with her family. Now, living in this same house is their nephew Lynn.

To the left was a musket dime and plum patch. As you come down the road, you could see fields of watermelon patches, hay, and peanut patches. There was a small hill just before reaching the house. There was a tree on the left just before coming up the small hill to the house; just past the tree were white rubber tires filled with flowers Momma had planted. She had a beautiful flower garden. The white rubber tires helped to bring out the color of the flowers. As you can see she had a love for flowers. Just past the flower garden was a big shade tree. This is where she had a bed with springs, chairs, more flowers, and picnic tables.

The property was surrounded and protected with barb wire fences. This was for the animals to stay within the pastures. And to help keep protection around the gardens and fruit trees. There were times the animals escaped the barn yard. Most of all this helped to divide the property line.

I can recall my brothers helping my dad repair the fences on many of occasions. There were days they cut the bushes to help keep the property clear. Cut wood for the winter months to fill the heaters.

Barn

To the left, south of the big shade tree were the barn and a pasture for the cows and mules to run. West of the shade tree was where the car shed was located. It seems as though daddy did not keep the car in the shed very often. This was the shed that Cody and I killed bumble bees with a bat for a game. Whoever killed the most would win. Also, this was where I panicked when I saw a brown snake curled up in the corner upper shelf of the shed. We kept cotton in this shed after picking. We weighed the cotton on the side where the car would sometimes be parked.

To the right of the shed was where the house was located. Between the shed and the house was a road that led you to the fields. We had a tree house off this road down behind the house. There were fishing spots, vines to swing on, corn and cotton fields. There were swimming spots to swim. Blackberry vines, crab apple trees, and walnut trees were located down in this area. We called this area the bottom. My cousins had their fields near our fields. Our house overlooked the direction of the highway and Aunt Lil's house. Right in front was a fruit orchard with apples and peaches that Grandpa had planted. There was a pear tree to the left of the house. Below the orchard was our vegetable garden, peanut patch, cantaloupe and watermelon patch.

Hog

Next to the house on the left was the water well. Past the well was the chicken house. To the east of the chicken house and west of the house some feet away was an outhouse. Just past the back of the house on the left was the smokehouse, where we stored the meat (pork) for the winter months. Each winter we killed a hog. We were raised on pork, chickens, rabbits, squirrels, coons, and opossum. We never killed the cows. We needed them alive for our milk and butter.

There was a plenty of hunting that took place for survival. Many foods were canned, salted down and stored for the cold winter months. In the summer we relied on chicken and other animals along with the fruit and vegetables. And there were fishing times. It was something we all enjoyed doing. Fresh fish was part of the meals as well. Country ham was a real treat with biscuits and homemade molasses. We made our own maple syrup as well. The corn was taken to a mill for grinding to make our cornmeal for cornbread.

Porch swing

The house was painted white with dark green trimming. The porch consisted of two dark green swings that sat one on each end of the porch. Momma had ivy plants hanging from the banisters.

As you entered the house, there was the living room. This room consisted of a couch on the left. There was a stove top heater in the middle of the floor that took fire wood to burn and a big wall mirror set on the right of the room opposite of the couch.

Behind the mirror was where Momma kept several of her business papers. It used to be a bed that Momma and Daddy slept in by the front window. This was only while so many children were still living at home. This was later moved into the first bedroom on the right, which was Momma and Daddy's bedroom.

After leaving the living room, straight back was a bedroom. It had two full-size beds on the left side of the room and a shift row with a long mirror for storing clothes on the right side of the room. There was a small wooden-frame couch and a dresser with a mirror on the same side of the shift row. There was a back door leading to the backyard.

Off from the living room on your right, again, was where Daddy and Momma slept. There were two full-size beds on the north side of the room. On the south side of the room was a dresser. And behind the door was where clothes were hung.

In the kitchen, as you walk in from Momma and Daddy's bedroom, on the left, there was a cabinet, stove, and refrigerator. At the back of the kitchen was a table. Across from the stove and cabinet was a dinner table. Against the wall opposite of the bedroom wall was a freezer. On the right of the room, just below the dinner table, was an exit door to the smokehouse and water well. On the opposite side to the end of the room, there was another exit door leading to the back porch.

This was the room, the kitchen, where all the homemade dishes and canning took place. And at the dinner table, you found things funny but would not dare to laugh while eating. And the living room was the fun room. It was where all the scary stories, jokes, company with their stories, and plain old conversations took place. My brothers and I played a game called goods. This is where you take a book and find the word good or goods in it. We shared the book in order for the game to be played. Each time you find a word a point was given to that person. The single word good was worth one point. The plural word goods were worth five points. It was family time in the living room and family time at the dinner table. We were all together. This house was filled with full bellies, a lot of love, and prayers.

We may have struggled, but we had pretty much of what we needed to survive and less than half we wanted. The most dangerous things we dealt with were snakes, mad dogs, quicksand, and someone leaving the mental institution. It wasn't so much the mentally ill would hurt us. It was because we were afraid and we would most likely hurt ourselves because we were afraid.

Afraid is an understatement. I was afraid of any and everything after dark. At the new place, we lived out in the country about ten miles away from town where we did most of the business. We lived off Highway 125 onto a dirt road. The nearest town was Middleton. It was about six miles away. The first house you saw was that of Aunt Lil. We were the last house on the place. This is the house Grandpa lived in and gave to Momma after we lost the old place.

It was a peaceful place. Many times, we made our own fun. When we were growing up, we thought that people had it better than us. And many did have it better. But there were many who did not.

I remember as a teenager thinking, if I had a boyfriend to come out to court me, he would need a magnifying glass and a helicopter to find me. Now that I look back, it really wasn't so bad. I can appreciate and enjoy the peace and quiet now that I am older.

We took the school bus to school every day. We had to walk down the dirt road all the way to the highway. It was a little better than a quarter of a mile. And, still, this wasn't as far as my elder sisters and brothers had to walk.

In the spring and summer months we walked down the dusty country road to the main highway to catch the school bus. There were days when I arrived at school my legs, hair, and clothes felt dusty. In the winter months daddy put hot coals from the heater in a pal for my brothers to carry with us in order for us to keep warm. We had a little wooden house there with the windows out. This was for us to stand in until the bus came. There were times we made a fire for that same reason. The bus was late often. We put out the fire when we saw the bus coming. Entering the bus with the smell of smoke in our hair and clothes wasn't something that was desired by other students; I'm sure. But I never had anyone say anything about the smell.

In my first ten years, I attended school at an all—African American school. This school Bolivar Industrial Elementary and Bolivar Industrial High School were located around ten miles from where we lived.

At night we had programs at school and we rode the bus. The bus driver was a very nice man who loved children. His name was Mr. Jones. It was dark when we got home after the programs. One night they had a drawing. Momma was the winner of a large box of towels. She was so happy. When we get off the bus all we had was moonlight and the stars to guide us home. But it was still a real treat.

At the end of the school day, Momma had dinner ready for us. And during that time, dinner may consist only of a pot of hominy. Boy, it was the best! The weather was cold. We were cold. And the hominy was good and hot. When we went to bed at night, we slept soundly and did not hear a thing.

On Saturdays, the family went to town. Momma stayed in the car much of time. We had a buffalo fish, bologna, or hamburgers for dinner after returning home from the trip. I say trip because of the distance from town. When the children had swallowed a fish bone; Momma gave them a slice of bread to eat. This bread was to wrap the bone so it did not stick you or get hung.

When we attended church or just sit at the table eating, it was very hard to stop laughing when something was funny. We quite often would almost burst out with laughter until Daddy cuts his eyes at us, and his jaws start moving. It was as if he already had us in the fields picking cotton. We would cut the laugh off like a light switch.

Speaking of eating at the table, when Daddy was eating, many times he pointed to what he wanted on the table. He ate so fast. Sometimes, he would just say Momma's name and motion with his head in the direction of the item he wanted on the table, and momma passed him the dish. For some reason manners did not appear to be an issue.

Daddy's hunger from working so hard in the fields stood in the way of him being polite at the table. He rushed to finish so he could go back to the fields. There wasn't any time to waste. After all the years Momma and Daddy had been together, they seem to have understood one another, and the love showed. They had a special bond.

I recall Momma sitting on the porch in the chair eating buttermilk and corn bread out of a bowl. She had her big toes on each foot turned up without shoes on. She opened her mouth rather wide with each spoonful.

Daddy was sitting in the swing on the porch, and I was sitting next to him. He was cutting his eyes over at Momma. Finally, he said, "Wesley B., now, I know it must be awfully good; but I don't think you are going to miss your mouth."

They laughed together and often sit on the porch swing at night together as well. One of them would make a smoke out of old rags to keep away the mosquitos. They had to or they would have been eaten alive by the mosquitos.

Children will be children. I can recall; one time, Momma was going to whip me. She swung at me and lost her balance. She didn't fall, but it frightened me. She was a full figured woman. I begged her to whip me after that, not only because I was afraid of her falling, but had she told Daddy, I probably would have gotten in trouble.

He did not want us to worry her in anyway. In the past we worried momma, many times, begging for what we knew we could not afford and places we knew she would not let us go and needed to go. All she had to say was "I'm going to tell your daddy." The begging ceased. And don't let Daddy walk in! It would be like E.F. Hutton; everybody listened. I know it sounds harsh.

In today's standards, this would be considered child abuse, the way our parents raised us and the way their parents raised them. Our parents did what they thought was right at that time and what was taught to them by their parents. Even with the discipline, I think we all know that they loved and protected us. None of us ended up in gangs or in jail. Most of all, we learned the word respect and honesty and what it really meant. We as children did a plenty mischievous things.

Our teachers as well as our parents paddled us when they felt we needed to be disciplined. I came up in the era when spanking was allowed and it was not called child abuse.

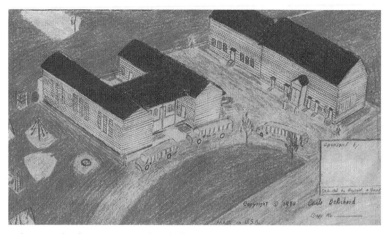

Bolivar Ind. Elementary School Illustrated by Carlo De-Richard Woods

My third grade was a grade to be remembered. My elementary school was a wooden frame school I attended. It had a long porch across the front. My teacher Ms. Lake wrote our

Bolivar Industrial School Alma mater. She taught on one end of the porch while Mrs. Anderson taught at the other end. Their class rooms were a straight aim from each other. Our principal was Mr. Rivers. The elementary school stopped at the end of the sixth grade. I looked forward to recess every day. The childhood games and the playground were fun each time. Teachers were pretty strict. They taught you not only as a teacher but as if they were your parent. The word respect defiantly was re-enforced. During this time teachers and parents were together on the children learning, behavior, and wellbeing.

There were some teachers I thought improperly used their authority when it came time for disciplining the children in their classroom. I witnessed paddling by other teachers that were a little too harsh. I and two other female classmates had a paddling from Ms. Lake. One afternoon we were to wait on the porch for the school bus per Ms. Lake. Neither one of us obeyed. I'm sure it did not cross my mind nor my classmates mind that if we missed the bus, Ms. Lake was responsible for us getting home. Neither one lived very close to the school. My classmates were closer than me. I was ten miles away. Therefore missing the school bus would have created a problem. We decided we were going to play and run around away from the porch. Ms. Lake grabbed the paddle come here she says.

You know there are some things you would like to forget. Anyway I should have gotten my paddling first. The other classmates went on and gotten theirs. But I was the last one. As the bus turned in off the road onto the elementary school entrance, I was getting my paddling finished on the porch. She was swinging and yelling out don't let the bus leave Mable.

Everyone on the bus saw me get that paddling. I think my pride was hurt more than the paddling. As I entered the bus, everyone was looking at me. Somehow I do not recall the pain as much as the embarrassment. There was a girl in upper class on the bus. She moved over for me to have a seat with her. I was looking really pitiful. She had a candy bar in her hand. As she began to peel the paper back, I stared her down and the candy bar even more until she broke me off a piece. That seemed to have helped the paddling situation.

Today's society will look at it differently. I can recall my brother saying one of his teachers was paddling him and quoted saying, "I whip you because I love you" He said in his mind, "I wish you didn't love me so much."

Momma and Daddy use to say, "A hard head makes a soft behind." They were right. One evening, I wanted to do my homework for school. Momma was over to Aunt Lil's (her sister) house. Daddy and Freddie were headed down the hill toward the front to cut bushes.

Clinora was in the kitchen cooking. Everybody else called her Sis. I called her Soot. I was a little girl in grade school at the time. Picture an in-love sister with her head thrown back, singing the song, "Summer Time," loudly and out of tune.

In the meantime, I took a piece of paper and didn't twist it enough to light the wick on the coal oil lamp. The lamp sat near the wall. The flames caught the wallpaper in the living room. And the flames were getting close to the back of the mirror where Momma kept some business papers.

I walked calmly to the doorway of the living room and said, "Soot, the house on fire." She just kept singing "Summer time and the living is easy; fish are jumping, and the cotton is high."

Before she could sing, "Your daddy's is rich, and your momma is good looking," I yelled, "Soot, the house is on fire!"

Flames were getting bigger. She dropped everything and ran in the living room, on to the front door, yelling in excitement, "'Daddy, Freddie, the house on fire.'"

They dropped the axe and ran to the house. They put the fire out. When the fire was out, I looked at Freddie, and I looked at Clinora. Both of them walked away with their heads down. They went in different directions. Daddy went out the front door. I knew when Clinora and Freddie dropped their heads; it was time for some more fire.

Daddy came back into the house. I can't remember him fussing or yelling. But he had a switch so long; I thought he had pulled up a tree. He whipped me until I slid under the bed and got in the corner. And I cried as loud as I could and stayed in that corner until he got tired of swinging. I waited a long time, before I came out to make sure he was gone. That was the only whipping that I had ever received from my dad. I don't think he wanted to whip me. But the fear and thought of the fire brought on the action that was taken. Plus, it is my understanding he had already lost a sister in a house fire before.

I can understand that we could have lost everything. We had lost one place. I learned that "You do not play or mess around with fire—too dangerous. And do not mess with the other fire, your parents—too dangerous. And you do not tell an in-love sister—nothing important. "When I finally checked to see if the coast was clear, I started toward Aunt Lil's house where Momma was over there visiting. When she saw me coming, she started toward home. We walked back together.

The first thing I did when I saw her was cry. Momma said, "What's the matter with you?" Maybe I should have phrased this a little differently, but I replied, "Daddy whipped me."

Momma knew that it had to be something bad for Daddy to whip me. She asked so very calmly with a soft voice, "What did you do?" I told her I caught the house on fire. Well, I tell you, wrong answer if I was looking for sympathy. I couldn't get away with a lie with this because there would have been another whipping if I had lied.

Momma stated, "It's no better for you and kept walking." No love that day! As a child, you want that. Even though it was an accident, parents look at the big picture and the loss we would have had. We had already lost one house. We could not afford to lose another home, and where would we go!

Again, it is just not good to have a hard head. Carl and Clinora were picking blackberries. This was down below the front of the house by the vegetable garden. I went over to stick my hand in the bush to pick some blackberries. Now, they told me to come from over there. No, I wanted some blackberries.

I picked the top part of the bush. I continued down to approximately half way the bush. This is when my hand hit a wasp nest. The wasps were black like the berries. And the wasps traveled straight up my arms to my face. I screamed to the top of my lungs.

Carl and Clinora, one on each side of me, grabbed me by my arms, lifting me from the ground. They were picking the wasps off me. It was a wasp attack for sure. By the time we got to the house, both of my eyes were closed, and no, I did not go to the doctor. I just waited until the swelling went down. I remember sitting on Momma's lap, eating apples with closed eyes.

During my fourth grade year I had fun playing with my cousins. We did not do too much visiting. Time did not seem to allow us to do so. My parents were always working in the fields, cooking, canning, killing wild game, putting food up for the winter months, making quilts, and salting down the pork.

The family did not have much money. It had to be spared and back then doctors were not seen too often. For one thing, Momma and Daddy did not have the money for the doctor's visits. We did not have a hospital in town. We had to go to Jackson General Hospital in Jackson, Tennessee in the next county.

When we got hurt, they fixed it. We had credit with the Watkins man. She used liniment and salve for us many times along with their own home remedies.

I think back to when we had gone to town one Saturday. Momma stayed in the car. I skipped up the street on the way to the candy store. On my way, I caught the front of my right leg on the shin bone on Mr. Booker's car fender. It put a big gash in my leg. It was gashed down to the white meat. I cried big tears. Mind you, we were in town. I hopped back to the car bleeding and with skin hanging off. Momma said; what's the matter?" I told her I hit my leg on the car. She replied, "Put this rag on it. And I'll put something on it when I get home."

When we arrived back home, Momma cleaned it. She put some salve on it and wrapped it up. Later, I kept picking at it. It did not seem like it was going to heal fast enough, so I put some dirt on it. It finally made a scab on the sore and healed. I guess, sometimes, natural is better.

This was the year for my worms. And the ringworms on my face seem to linger on forever. Momma and Daddy began to worry about me. This was one time Momma took me to the doctor. My mom says to my dad these ringworms don't want to clear up. After a few trips to the doctor, some old lady told Momma to take some pure turpentine and rub on my naval and put a drop with some sugar in a glass of water and let me drink it. The sugar would draw the worms, and the turpentine would help bring them out when I went to the bathroom. Sure enough, as time went on, I passed the worms, and my face cleared up.

This summer also brought quite a surprise. It was hot this summer day. Momma had been to the garden to pick fresh green beans. Instead of going back inside the hot house she instructed me to bring a big bowl and our big cooking pot from the kitchen. She decided to sit under the first shade tree there in front of the house. While she was snapping the fresh green beans I was busy playing with my doll and our dog.

In the mist of snapping the beans she looked up. Somebody's coming says momma. I replied; I don't see anybody. She stood up. She put her hand across her forehead trying to block the sun ray as she looked across the hill of the old dusty road. The person was coming down the hill in our direction. Momma says "I know that walk." He became closer and she began to meet him. I heard her say the prodigal son. My mom being a heavy set woman, it did not matter to this man. He picked her up and held her so tight before letting go. He looked down at me. I was standing there looking up at him and wondering who he was while hiding behind momma's dress. She introduced him. "Child this is your brother Arthur." He left home when I was around three and I was now nine years old.

This is the brother my sister told me about. When he was growing up, he used to make fun of a man that walked with a limp. Momma told him "don't make fun of other people, because you might end up like them." Sure enough Arthur stepped off in a ditch and end up limping like the man for a long time. I guess it pays to listen to your parents.

I practically followed him around the whole time he was there. I can recall the loud smelling shaving powder he used for shaving. With each stroke he took a sip from this can. I was curious as usual about what he was drinking. He told me it was something I couldn't have. But I insisted on knowing what it was anyway.

He says go ahead and take a swallow. I see you are not going to listen to me. I decided not to take a little swallow in fear he would not let me have another. I took the biggest swallow I could. I began to feel light headed. The room was spinning. I decided to lie down on the sofa. With a relaxed body and slow slurred speech I asked; "what was that? My brother replied; beer something I told you that you didn't need.

The beer situation was just the beginning of this visit with my brother. I used to love sugar in my biscuits. I guess it was my way of it taking the place of candy. Momma told me on many occasions stay out of the sugar. One particular day when my brother was still visiting, Momma says in front of him, "Didn't I tell you to stay out of that sugar before you get sick?" "Yes momma!" I skipped down the hill with the dog at my side while eating my sugar and biscuit sandwich.

Later on that evening momma and daddy were sitting under the shade tree. My brother Arthur was getting dressed to visit someone in town. It was on a Saturday. I headed for the kitchen. He went through the back way and met me in the kitchen. Arthur says I know what you are in here for. I'll fix it for you. I waited but I wasn't watching. He handed me my sandwich. I made it to the front porch. It was then I took my first big bite. He had filled my biscuit full of salt. I yelled; out with a cry. I proceeded to the shade tree holding my salt biscuit in my hand. As I approached my mom and dad were laughing amongst themselves.

I told her that Arthur had put salt in my biscuit. Momma's reply; "I told you to stay out of the sugar." Needless to say it all sounded terrible what had happen between my brother and me. He gave me some tough love. Because of the tough love act, I never liked or drank beer again. And I never went back to get the sugar and biscuit sandwich. In this case the tough love paid off.

We enjoyed Christmas. As children, we would go out into the woods and cut a Christmas tree. Chopped wood was stacked up high on the porch for the winter. The house had an area around the door facing where the green trimming was located. We collected all the green branches with the little red hollies on it and put it all around the door. Once we got the tree up, we decorated the tree with strings of popcorn, little things we made, some of the greeting cards we had received, and garlands made out of paper. Boy we were excited! We did not have electricity at the time therefore we did not have strings of electric lights to go on the tree.

The cedar and the popcorn made the house smell so good. Momma and Daddy would go to town and get the big peppermint log candy, oranges, apples, and nuts. Christmas Eve momma and daddy had brown paper bags with our fruit and candy and nuts in it. We used the old pressing iron to crack some of the nuts. And we turned it upside down and used a hammer to crack them. Christmas morning we had our little gifts under the tree. My brother Carl traded his orange for an apple with his siblings because he says the acid in the orange left his teeth feeling funny.

Momma had the kitchen smelling good for a couple of days. She always made Daddy's favorite cakes coffee cake and coconut cake. And the chocolate cake was the best. She made icing as if you could go skating on it. It was smooth and rich.

One year, Momma had ordered me a ball-headed doll from the catalog. She kept looking for the mailman to bring it. But it did not get there in time for Christmas. She always tried to hide those things from you.

Momma waited until the last minute of Christmas Eve. She made sure that box showed up. Since the box did not come, Momma went to town to the five-and-dime store and found me the exact baby doll that was just like the one in the book. I was with her when she entered the five and dime store. She tried to pick the doll up with her back turned while I was looking at other toys. The clerk was willing to assist momma in hiding the doll from me. She made sure I had a doll for Christmas morning.

The next couple of days, the other doll came that she had ordered from the catalog. Therefore, I had twin dolls. Momma did not bother to return the doll back that she had ordered. I probably begged her to keep the second one.

As I think of baby dolls, I can't help but think of the babies that were being born of the same age in my family. When Momma was pregnant with me, she had a daughter (Idell), another daughter, Allie and a daughter-in-law, Bessie; pregnant the same time that she was pregnant. Cody was born first. I was born second, Regina, and then Gregory.

In the summer of my fifth grade year Cody my eldest sister's son visited. It was nice to have him with us. Allie did not have a baby sitter therefore; he spent the summer with us. Since Cody and I were the same age we become close. He had me about one month in age. He hung out with my brother's Carl and Carnell. All summer we had great fun. He liked it so much on the farm that he wanted to stay. He loved learning how to hunt and follow my brothers and learned whatever they taught him.

We had hunting dogs. I can remember when we were sitting under the big shade tree. Our dog Rock came from behind the house up the dirt road. He was walking with his head down and very slowly as if he could not make it up the hill. He finally reached the shade tree. We all looked and asked what was wrong with him.

Momma took one look and said, "He has been bitten by a snake. Now, go to the house, cut a piece of salt pork, split it in the middle down to the skin. Make sure you don't cut the skin now. Put the salt pork in the skillet and warm it up a little. And bring it down here and drape it across his nose."

I was worried that Rock was going to eat the meat. Momma said he will not eat it. Sure enough, he did not. I guess he was too sick to care. Momma said the salt would help draw the swelling. After a few days, he was up and running around again.

Old Hunter was a very smart and protective dog. He was pretty much all white with short hair. I can remember after Daddy, Carl and Carnell had finished with the hay, I asked if I could water the mule. They let me take old Dick down below the barn where the pond was located.

I was in front. I had him by the strap and not having a care in the world. Just before we got to the pond, Dick stopped. Apparently, someone else had been to the pond and got some water. I kept saying, "Come on, mule."

He kept bucking his head up and trying to back up. I just so happen to look down. There was a snake lying across the road path. It was a blessing that I did not step on the snake. I yelled at the top of my lungs, "Snake!" By this time, Dick had raised up on his hind legs with his two front feet in the air.

Out of the clear blue came Hunter. He had some speed on him. He grabbed the snake behind his head and shook him up against the tree and the barbed wire fence before he let go. Boy, he was the first thing on the scene. My brothers followed hunter.

Thank god for old Dick and old Hunter. They saved my life. I couldn't ask for a better set of animals than those two. I guess you can say, if you care about animals, they will care about you. This goes for people too.

During this summer my cousins, Ruthie and Ruby and I had gone to Grandpa's house. We walked over the long dusty road bypassing the cemetery. Somehow, my knee locked up. It was very painful; I couldn't let it down. It was getting late in the evening. Grandpa told Ruthie and Ruby to get my parents. They took off running.

We did not have a telephone at the time nor did Grandpa. It was beginning to get dark. Finally Momma and Daddy came in their 1946 black Ford. I can recall hopping into the car. When we arrived home, Daddy picked me up and carried me into the house on his hip. I could see the concern he had. And I appreciate compassion he showed.

A few months later while having breakfast, Daddy stopped talking in the middle of his sentence. We were all at the table. Everyone ate at the same time in this house. Momma knew something was wrong right away. She looked at him and called his name, "Arthur! Arthur!" All he did was raised his eyebrows a couple of times. I guess he thought he had sound coming from his mouth; but indeed, there were none.

Daddy aroused from the table and walked behind their bedroom door. He was a handsome and tall, dark, with salt-and-pepper hair. Momma stood shorter than him. She looked up into daddy's face with such love and care. She reached behind his head and rubbed it. She turned and told Cody and I to go call Clinora and the doctor down at our neighbor's house, the Howell family.

We later found out that he had a blood clot to pass through. Daddy would have awful nose bleeds. And, sometimes, it would last quite a while. I have seen him from time to time get down on one knee while his nose was bleeding. It was a good thing he had the bleeds because it helped to release some of the pressure. Both my parents suffered with high blood pressure.

When summer ended Cody still wanted to live with us. I was going to enter the sixth grade in the fall. Cody entered the fifth grade because of the changing of the schools from state to state. He did not mind. He still wanted to live with us.

By the time I reached sixth grade, I was getting prepared for high school for the next year. I was a little nervous. I was wondering how I was going to fit in. I had an elder sister and two brothers in Bolivar Industrial High. What stands out the most about my sixth grade year was my teacher, Mrs. Horton and the bee. Mrs. Horton was a tall slim lady with skin pigmentation. She had this inner beauty that was very noticeable. I thought she was an unbelievably kind and easy going teacher. I could relax and learn with her. Outside of those big windows without any screens was a nice tall honey suckle bush. It sat in the corner outside the classroom. I recall standing next to it and a bumble bee flew in my hair. I could hear the bee buzzing. I tried to brush him out with my hands. He stung my head. A big lump came under the skin. I remember thinking that it will never go down. And I wondered if I was going to the seventh grade with this big lump on my head.

Regardless of all the children my dad had, he loved his nephews. This was his blind and eldest sister's children. He helped his nephews Ernest and Earl build homes. They built Daddy's friend, Mr. Booker Shelly's new house. Momma would sometimes go down and stay with his wife, Mrs. Shelly, while Daddy worked.

Momma told me that morning, "Get off the school bus after school with their daughter, Joanne." We were in the same grade and still in elementary school then.

Daddy would come home and tell some of their jokes that he heard while they were working together. Just a wonder, Mr. Booker's house didn't fall in. They were having so much fun and Daddy loved every bit of it. But the house is still standing today.

Looking back to when my mom and I visited Detroit. We took a trip over to Ohio to visit my sister Eunice. This was when I met little Freddie for the very first time. He is the son of my brother Freddie. Little Freddie was still in diapers.

Momma fell in love with him and asked if she could take him back with her. His mom hesitated for quite a while there. Momma kept talking, and, finally, she packed up his things. She was a single mom and also was having a hard time. Once she agreed to let little Freddie come home with us, you would think Momma had gotten a Christmas gift.

We returned back home to the country. Daddy, Cody, and I fell in love with him too. He had a little red tricycle that he had rode so much that all the wheels were wobbly. And the tricycle was leaning to one side. He would get so angry at the tricycle. He used to pick up a stick and demand it to straighten up. When he got it straight enough, he got on it and rode until he turned a corner and falls off of it again. He was tough and took charge, even at that age.

Momma combed my hair. Cody and I dressed for church. She dressed little Freddie. Boy, he was well dressed. He'd have on a white suite, white high top shoes, white shirt, and a white bow tie. He looked better than all of us. It did not matter how much or how hard we worked. We still had time for church.

My dad worked so hard in the fields. I can recall Momma calling me to take him some water in a mason fruit jar. She would tell me, "Come here and draw some fresh water from the well and take to your daddy."

I walked down to the field. On the way, I could hear something crawling in the weeds along the side of the road. Sometimes, I ran across a lizard, a sand skitter, or even a snake. Once I get to the fields, I was shaking in my shoes because I was afraid of everything when I was alone.

There, Daddy was walking behind one of the mules in the hot sun. He had on a long-sleeve shirt, straw hat, overalls, and high top shoes. I walked over where he was. It did not matter if he was in the middle of the row or at the end. He took the water and drank it straight down without stopping. He did not care if it was cold, he just wanted it wet.

Daddy was wringing wet with sweat, and dirt built up on his skin from the dusty plowing of the field. I think back at how hard he worked in those fields and Momma too. He walked behind the mules step by step from sun up to sun down. He'd stop long enough for dinner. At that time we called lunch at twelve O'clock dinner. In the evening we called dinner supper. Now that I am older I can look back and say with all the things my parents did to provide for us, how could we not appreciate it?

Bolivar Industrial High School

I was beginning my high school this year. When I was growing up we often referred to the elementary school the old building and the high school the new building. Bolivar Industrial High is now known as the Junior High school. The School was known as the home of the Red Devils and Deviletts. In 1957 the school was built. They opened the doors in 1958. In 1961 there were about 52 graduating students that year. Many remembered how proud the school principal, Professor Miller was. The last graduating class before the schools were integrated was in 1970. Serving as the Deputy Director of Hardeman County Board of Education is Mr. Bobby Doyle. The director of the Learning Center is Mr. Thomas Polk.

Entering the seventh grade year, the one teacher that I can remember most was Ms. Johnson. She was our music teacher. I must say I passed the class but could not draw some of the music notes on the music sheet. She used to tell a student if, "you can talk, you can sing." Passing in the halls were something different than in the grade school. But, no one got out of line. We were like little soldiers. The high school principal stood in the middle of the hall holding one arm with his hand. For a long time I thought my principal was white. He kept things in line during the time I spent in Bolivar Industrial High.

Momma and Daddy suffered from high blood pressure. I think back to how momma relied on Anacin for pain. And daddy believed in ben-gay for pain. He figured rubbing it on his temper would help. The only aid to their blood pressure problems were the Anacin tablets to help thin the blood. And money was an issue for their medical problems. I often wonder how much the salted down pork and hot sun played in their blood pressure problems. Daddy would continue to have his nose bleeds in the summer months. And in the winter he had leg pain.

Growing up we certainly tried Daddy. We had to learn that there was one thing you could not do with Daddy, and that was to make a bet with him. I was twelve years old. We had to pick cotton at someone else's field. I bet Daddy that I could pick two hundred pounds of cotton. He bet me two dollars that I couldn't.

We started out super early the next morning for the field. I was determined to win this bet with my dad. I wasn't serious about the bet at the beginning. But I had opened my big mouth. I worked really hard. Each time I went to the scale to weigh my cotton sack it would only be about twenty five or thirty pounds. We only sat down to eat lunch and go to the bathroom which consisted of going into the woods behind a tree. It was getting close to time to stop working at the end of the day. I needed only twenty nine pounds to win the bet. I was really tired at this point. I was about to give up when my brother said you can do it. I was almost at the end of the cotton row when the man we were working for says "quitting time." I walked slowly to the scales.

My brother's cotton was weighed first. I was afraid for them to put my sack on the scale. The man weighed my cotton sack. He kept fooling around with the scale adjusting it to get the exact weight. I was sitting on the ground looking up. He finally came up with a weight. He says the total weight is thirty one pounds knocking of two pounds off for the weight of the sack itself. My sack was smaller than my brother's. The larger sacks had three pounds knocked off for the weight. The smaller sacks weight had two pounds knocked off for its weight. This gave me exactly the twenty nine pounds I needed to win the bet.

It was hard to do. But I won the bet. My brothers were happier than I was. As we were walking home from the highway, Carnell and Carl said, "Walk slow and act like you didn't pick that much." I wanted to tell Daddy that I picked two hundred but the boys told Daddy, "She picked 200!" He gave me the two dollars but told me I better pick two hundred in his field the next day.

I just didn't have it in me the next day. We went to church that night. I purchased two bologna sandwiches for a dime each. Momma kept up with the money. She could see I was going to spend it all on food and get sick. I guess it did not make sense for both of us to be up all night with me getting sick.

By the time I entered my eighth grade year I was in for something I was not prepared for. And it changed my whole life. During the summer leading up to the school year, I remember having loads of fun with my brothers and my two cousins. Of course, fun was with my cat and dogs as well. I had already turned 13 in the spring. My brother Carnell was fifteen. I have always considered Cody as my brother. He was also thirteen years old.

During my eighth grade year I had a crush on a boy that attended our school. He took a shop class. My cousin was his teacher. And his dad was one of the school janitors at the school. All the boy and I could do was wave at each other. He was in the first semester of his tenth grade year and attended a different school while being bussed to our school for a shop class. There weren't any telephone calls between us.

There are things we cannot change in life. But when you are hit with a complete surprise, you kind of wonder why now?

As the bright ceiling lights shined in my face, I began to complain, "Daddy, turn out the light," as I tossed and turned for a few minutes. I repeated, "Daddy, turn out the light!" It was before midnight on October 1, 1965. I slept on the sofa in the living room that particular night. I covered my head with the covers, trying to avoid the light in the ceiling.

Then, I heard the voice of Daddy saying, "Baby! Your Momma had a stroke!" I jumped to my feet from the sofa. I ran to their bedroom doorway. Daddy had a wet cloth, sponging Momma off.

I ran to my brother's bedroom (Carnell and Cody) and yelled with a shaky voice, "Daddy said Momma had a stroke." My brother's jumped to their feet. They also ran to the doorway of Momma and Daddy's bedroom.

Daddy told them, "You boys go down to Sam Howell's and have them call the doctor and call Sis (Clinora)." We did not have a telephone at the time. And Clinora lived and worked in the next town (Toon, Tennessee). And the Howell family lived across the road down on the highway where we catch the school bus. Daddy looked so pitiful; so did we.

It seemed forever for the doctor and Clinora to get there. At the time that my brothers were gone, I walked to the side of Momma's bed. She was having some fluid come out of her mouth.

I got an empty corn can and put it to her mouth. Her hand lightly clasping over my hand and, all of a sudden, she let go. I'll never forget that touch and the helpless feeling I had at that moment. I was looking at the hurt and uneasiness in Daddy. At age thirteen, I was in disbelief and not really understanding too much at the time. It was all a shock to us.

Finally, the boys came back home. The doctor arrived, and so did Clinora. The doctor examined Momma. It is my understanding that the doctor told Daddy and Clinora that it was the second highest blood pressure that he had ever taken. She had indeed had a stroke. It was told to me later that Daddy said Momma woke him up and told him, "Arthur, I think I'm having a stroke!"

They had Momma transported by ambulance to Jackson General Hospital in Jackson, Tennessee. This was in the next county. Once at the hospital, we learned that the stroke had destroyed all five senses. She was in a coma. And if she was to live, she would only be a vegetable.

The other sisters, brothers, uncles, aunts, and Grandpa were contacted. And they came to visit Momma.

The waiting was rather hard on everyone. Of course, everyone was waiting for some kind of good news. But I guess the good news was more or less hope. This makes me think back at something Momma had said before she had gotten sick. She did not want to suffer. And God answered her prayers.

All the sisters and brothers came from Detroit and Cleveland. They took turns in pairs, at night, at the hospital while the others stayed at the house. When one pair leaves home, they would relieve the pair that was at the hospital. We would look for the car lights to top the hill off the highway.

Grandpa visited Momma (his daughter). It is my understanding; he walked into the hospital room to the foot of Momma's bed. He felt her feet and noticed her feet were cold and said, "Goodbye, daughter!"

Allie was telling me when Momma had her stroke, how she and Idell had gone to the hospital and talked with the doctors. They wanted to move Momma out of Jackson General and move her to Memphis or Detroit. The doctors told them, "You can move her anywhere you want to, but she will never utter another word or even know you."

It was the worse stroke they had ever seen. At that point, they had accepted it. It was my understanding, her blood pressure was the second highest that our family doctor, Dr. Bond, had ever checked.

Allie remembers one night before momma's death. She had slept on the floor under momma's bed and she heard all these footsteps. It woke her up. There were several doctors standing around her bed. She overheard some of the conversation.

The next morning she and our sister Ethel stopped by Aunt Addie's, Momma's elder brother's wife. She went on to tell her that she didn't think that they needed to go back because momma was dying. Aunt Addie says, "Don't say that!" You see back in August that summer of 1965, Momma felt that she was not going to live and told Allie that very thing. This stuck in Allie's mind what our mom had told her.

Allie was right. Momma got her blessing from God. She said that she did not want to suffer if she had gotten sick. She was in a coma.

On the third night, Daddy slept on his back in his overalls. This was very unusual for him to do. Three sisters were home in the back bedroom with me. For some reason, I started to sweat, had chills, and was running off. I just got deathly sick.

My sister Eunice asked another sister, "Do you think I should give her one of my nerve pills?" They said, "No, you better not do that." This went on for a little while.

Someone said, "I see a car light coming. I guess they are relieving the other ones." Then someone else said, "No, there are two sets of car lights. My sisters and brothers knew it couldn't have been good news.

When they got out of the car and the four walked in, they shook their heads from side to side and told everyone in the living room, "She's gone; she didn't make it!"

It's a funny thing; all my sickness went away. I often wondered if I was given some kind of sign of Momma's death at the time she was dying and if Daddy was given some kind of sign, the reason he slept in his overalls that particular night of all nights. All I know was my sickness was gone, and so was my momma. She lived for three days after her stroke.

At this point, they were trying to get together and figure out who would tell Daddy the news. Allie was crying and said, "I just can't tell him." It was finally decided that Clinora would be the one to tell him.

She walked to Daddy's bedside as he lay there in his overalls on his back. Touching his hand to wake him to give him the bad news, Clinora said to Daddy, "Daddy, the doctors done everything that they could. Momma didn't make it."

At this point, everyone was trying to hide their tears from Daddy. But we couldn't hold it back any longer. Daddy grabbed his chest as if he was having a heart attack or trying to pull his heart out. And all he could say was "ump, ump, ump; why didn't he take me!"

In the meantime, my elder brother Arthur had just driven back to Detroit to go back to work while Momma was still in the hospital. As soon as he reached Detroit, he got the news of her passing and had to turn around and come back for the funeral. Someone told me that Arthur stuffed his handkerchief in his mouth to keep from crying out at the funeral.

Even though Carnell (about age fifteen) and my nephew Cody (thirteen) stayed it still was an empty, lonely lost feeling. With Carnell, Cody and I being of age, we were able to still help Daddy in the fields and around the house.

And living with us a short time was little Freddie. Since he was around two years old when my mom passed we could not take care of him. After the funeral his dad took him back to Detroit and later back to Cleveland where his mom lived.

At the cemetery, he looked back at the casket with such a confused look as if to say, "what are they going to do with my grandma?'

After Momma died, Daddy was there raising a thirteen year old daughter, a fifteen year old son, and a thirteen year old grandson alone. He probably could deal with raising a boy as opposed to raising a girl. Momma was there to teach and ease the blow on a lot of things. Not just for Daddy but for me as well. He was not only learning to continue to be a parent all alone but a momma too. Even though Daddy had been hard and stern in the past, he softened up some after Momma died.

Clinora lived with us for a short time after Momma's death. One night, in the living room, she was trying to help me with my homework. I just wasn't paying attention and couldn't or didn't concentrate. She was so upset with me. Clinora yelled, "I am going to knock you on your tail if you don't pay attention."

Daddy rose up from his bed. Clinora said she thought she was going to get in trouble with Daddy. Mind you, she was grown and working then. After Daddy rose up from his bed, he said, "I wish you would knock her on her behind." Only he didn't use that word—this was a substitute for a stronger word, which was not like him.

It took a long, long, time to come down off the death of Momma. It seemed as though everything from the farm, the house, school, flowerbed, shade trees, everything was such a reminder of her. I felt stripped. I am sure it was hard for everyone else. But they had her growing up to kind of smooth things over when things got tough. And I know it was hard for Daddy because Momma handled the girls. Cody was still there, which was great company for me and very helpful to Daddy.

After my mom's death I had to grow up and get responsible and prepare myself for whatever future I was going to have. This meant I had to be determined to study much more and remember what I was taught. There were some low points at times.

I had been discouraged about things in my life when I was growing up that I could not understand. It seemed as though the life had been sucked right out of my body. I had to take deep breaths, collect my thoughts, pick myself up and keep moving. It was not easy. I had to learn early. You cannot let someone else control and stop what you are thriving for. I guess it is more or less like a ball game. You are in it to win it. You might have to sit on the bench for a while but you regroup get back in the game and give it all you have. Even if you do not win at least you can give yourself credit for putting forth an effort. If you do not put forth an effort then the other person will be the winner every time.

We all probably have experienced this one. Keep quiet! Have you ever known anyone that has been mistreated or misguided and the other person do not want you to speak up for yourself? If you do that it brings some light to the reason you are speaking out. It does not matter how wrong they could have been or how much of a difference if any they made in the process. Quiet now, let us move on they would say. While fixing part of the problem but want you to remain silent. You see fixing the surface of a problem is not really fixing the problem. Fixing the root of it would be more practical. Finding out some truth verses a lie would be a good beginning. It is not that people are forgetting you have feelings. What they are forgetting is that the damage has been done and what you think does not matter. They want to brush it under the rug so to speak. I ask myself is silence really golden? I would think that it depends on the situation and what and who is involved

In my ninth grade year my physical education teacher became my mentor. She was a rather young teacher and single at the time. She was a stern but caring person. She taught us so much about our personal hygiene and encouraged the female students to take pride in their body. I learned a lot about fallout shelter and parts of the body.

I recall a test in her class where we had to learn all the bones. I was very interested in it. I was seated at the back of the class. On test day Miss Ross walked up and down every row of her classroom. This was one time I was confident in a test. After the testing was over we passed over our papers. Top test scores will be on the board in a couple of days says Miss Ross. Sure enough Thursday or Friday that week came the top ten scores. They were placed on the black board. These were the scores of the ninth graders through the twelfth graders. I ranked number three from the top. My mind went back to my mom. I knew she would have been so very proud.

I played volleyball in school during our gym class. This was part of the class activity. Center front was the position I pretty much held. The gym was still located at the old elementary school. The students had to walk back to the high school a few feet away. My cousin Earl had his shop class on the first floor. The boy that liked me was still in his class.

Sometimes another classmate and I would finish our exercises before the others in the class. When this boy seen us coming, I could see through the window as he approached the teacher's desk and headed for the door, apparently asking the teacher to be excused. When we walked in the side door by the class room of the school he came from the water fountain. Cousin Earl stood at the doorway of his classroom.

My friend would whisper I'll call you. He called me in the evenings at 5pm on the dot. He did not have a telephone so he walked to his neighbor's house to use their telephone. He lived in a different town than me. There wasn't any dating involved. Plus he never learned how to drive. Even if he did drive daddy was strict. It probably would not have made much difference anyway. Momma had been gone a year. Much later daddy loosened up but this was after my friend graduated and joined the marines. I did not go places too much anyway. Most of our communication was by letters.

Daddy still had his set rules. He was the kind of father who made you respect the family and not want to bring shame to his home. Daddy raised his children the way he was raised. It might have been what we thought a little too rough. But he did what he was taught to do. He was a firm believer in "Your word is your bond." It means if you lie, you cannot be trusted.

Carnell went into the service. Cody and I hit it pretty hard in helping out around the house and the fields. The older siblings had gone back to their lives. Clinora was a big help to us because she lived in the next town. She later moved on to Detroit as well.

Age sixteen was a touchy point in my life. Growing older and growing up was something I had to learn the difference in. One Sunday evening, Daddy had to pick me up from over ten miles from a girlfriend's house. And I had school the next day. I was told by my friend that her momma was going to bring me home.

Well, we played and clowned around until it got dusk dark. We were both on the baseball team. I asked my friend about her momma taking me home. When she asked her mom, her mom said, "My truck lights don't work." This is where it began to sink in. I knew at that point I had to be more responsible. I should have had a better plan.

God had to have been in what was about to happen because I could have possibly found somebody to drop me off at the highway near the road up to our house. But it did not cross my mind at the time.

This forced me to make a telephone call to Daddy. He trusted me. I felt as though I let him down as well as myself. Ring! Ring! Ring! On the other end; Hello! Daddy can you come get me? "I thought her momma was bringing you home." Her truck-lights aren't working on her truck" I heard a dial tone. I knew he was hot under the collar. I waited nervously. Daddy came on to pick me up. No words were spoken all the way home between us. I knew it was better for me not to say anything. When Arthur was silent, you knew something was to come.

I knew he was steaming. He had traveled over about twenty miles round trip. Gas was very valuable. Off the highway we turned, onto the dirt road heading to the house. There were still no words spoken.

He pulled up under the first shade tree in front of the house. He parked the car. Still no words were spoken.

We got out of the car. I walked up the couple of steps first, onto the porch. Still no words were spoken. I opened the door. I entered the living room with Daddy on my heels. He was behind me the whole time. I mean close and very close behind me.

When I stepped just inside the door, I could feel his hot breath on the back of my neck. Still no words were spoken. I was afraid of what was about to come. Therefore, I took a couple of steps to the left away from him. This was just in case he started swinging.

He began to fuss. He said to me, "The next time you go somewhere, you better make sure you got a ride home." And he went on and on. With a kind of loud and shaky voice, I said, "I know one thing; I sure do miss Momma." He yelled at the top of his lungs with a trembling voice, "Don't you think I miss her too?"

I thought it to be anger, but, instead, it was hurt that I heard in his voice. Without thinking, because of my own loneliness of missing my mother, I did not think of my dad's feelings at the time.

At this point in your teenage life, especially for a girl, you figure a mother would be more understanding. Anger stood in the way of hurt before words were spoken. How can you not have compassion for your dad? After all, he had Momma much, much longer than I.

I started out the front door. He yelled again! "Where are you going?" I replied, "I am going to pee." What can I say? He frightened me! We did not have an indoor bathroom. In the past, I was always afraid of the dark but not this particular night.

As I walked outside, I began to cry. Missing my mother was an understatement. After the crying stopped, I began to think heavily on Daddy. I was being selfish about my own feelings. What about his?

Each person handles love, pain, and grief differently. How can we expect to know what the next person feels? All we do know is how we feel and have sympathy to the next person's feelings. Most of all we know at some point in our lives we all hurt. Sometimes we can express it and sometimes we are at a loss for words.

I've heard the expression, "death is so final." I have always believed that the physical body dies. Love lives in the hearts and memories of the people your body leaves behind making the person that left you somehow are still with you.

After going back into the house and into my bedroom, I felt as if Momma was looking down on both of us. I could just hear her saying to me, "Go to bed, now, child; everything is going to be all right," and to Daddy, "Now, Arthur, it will be all right in the morning," while rubbing the back of his head as she had always done.

I think this is what broke the ice for both of us. We were both hurting and missing Momma on this day as well as other days. I think he may have cried too at some point.

Momma had been gone about a year now. And one day, I came from the kitchen. I had just finished cooking. I was going to tell Daddy dinner was ready. As I walked to the living room, I could see Daddy sitting in the swing through the front window. Just as I approached the window, going to the door, I could see Daddy with one of Momma's perennial flowers in his hand. These are flowers that come back year after year without replanting them.

So I stopped for a minute. He must be thinking of Momma and missing her as I was too. When he turned his head, just enough for me to see his face; tears were lapping under his chin. I could see the pain he was in and it broke my heart.

I turned, went back through the bedroom, through the kitchen, and out the backdoor on to the backyard, and stopped by the smokehouse. And I cried like a newborn baby. It hurt me to my heart to see him cry that way. I couldn't fill that void. He was missing Momma some terrible.

After I got myself together, I tried again. This time, I yelled from the kitchen. "Daddy, dinner is ready!" This way, I would be giving him time to get himself together as well. He finally made it to the kitchen. It wasn't easy for either one of us.

Daddy and I managed to make it through our struggles. Losses can be painful and lonely but somehow you find the strength to overcome.

During the summer I visited Detroit. I stayed with my sister Idell and her family. Her daughter Regina and I were both born in the same month about eighteen days apart. I was born first.

I admired her. She had all the pretty clothes and a nice hair style. Here I was this poor old country girl. I was wishing I could have all the pretty things she had. This summer I arrived before she had gotten out of school for the summer break. I rode the city bus with her to Cass Tech High School. I probably was looking homely and possibly embarrassing to her. But my sister and her mom say you should go to school with Regina. Regina later told me she thought I had pretty hair and how pretty she thought I was. Once she was out of school we had fun together. She did not like the farm life. I did not expect her to understand the country life when she came to visit. I adjusted to the city life except for a couple incidents.

There were many things I did not know about the city. For example, I had never heard of a pizza or shrimp. And at first I did not like either one when I tasted them. The crust was the only thing I ate off the pizza.

I wrote my friends back home letters. I thought I mailed the letters. On the side of the street were a blue square mailbox and a blue square trash can. When my friends did not receive the letters I realized they were put in the trash can instead of the mailbox. I am glad I did not write a return letter to the President.

In my tenth grade year once again we had fun. Cody and I made our own fun. We did not have a basketball goal. We had the ball. But it did not have air. When we lost the ball we used old rags and stuffed it in an old sock. The goal was nailed to the back of the house. We used an old large tin can. I gave him a run for his money each time we played.

We should do what's right when it comes to our parents. Cody's mom would send him money home from time to time. Cody loved his honey buns. Now, we needed to do without some things for a while. This particular time, both of us had a little money in our pockets. Cody had taste for a honey bun. I had taste for Campbell's "ABC" soup.

Cody was always doing something crazy or funny. He had plenty of nerves. His little change was burning his pocket. We wanted to go to the store. We debated who was going to ask Daddy to take us. The store was little better than a mile from the highway. I was the one to ask Daddy to take us to the store. Well, he said, he needed to save his gas. I can recall how he used to cut the motor off when the car was on top of a hill. This was to save gas by letting the car coast down. After he made that statement about saving gas, I did not say anything else. I told Cody daddy said he had to save his gas for the car. So Cody convinced me to walk to Callahan store with him. We made it to the store and purchased what we were getting.

It was getting to be dusk dark. On our way back, Daddy met us on the highway. He went pass us and came back and slowed down. I'm thinking maybe he realized he needed something after all. Now that I think about it maybe he was feeling a little bad that he did not take us.

But Cody says to me, "Let's not get in if he stops." I was carefully listening to Cody. He was walking fast. But my mind was saying okay because Daddy had told me he needed his gas in his car. But my feet were saying something different.

We heard the car slow down almost to a complete stop. From the voice of Daddy came "Y'all want a ride?" We looked over at him in the car. Now, this was Arthur, our daddy, asking us if we wanted a ride.

I did not think twice. I jumped in the car. Cody jumped in right behind me. You see, I had sense enough to know, if we did not get in, Daddy might have gotten angry and gave us some chores and worked us a solid week. I did not want to work all week and pay for Cody's honey bun and my soup. Plus, I was glad he came along. I even offered Daddy some of my soup. He did not accept any.

There were times Daddy would drive his friend Mr. N.T. truck for him. He drove Mr. N.T.'s truck someplace for him one afternoon. Mr. N.T. did not seem to drive long distance or when it got dark.

When Daddy left home, Cody and I would get the mules and race them up the hill by Aunt Lil's house. Then we would put them back up. I can't remember if we watered the mules or not. I know that if Daddy had found out we raced the mules; he would have had a fit. If we raced them and did not water them, there would have been some action taken, like having knocked our knee caps off.

Of course, this was not satisfying to Cody. He had an itch to drive Daddy's car to Tate Doll's store that evening. His pocket was burning and his mouth was watering for another honey bun. Well, he asked me if I wanted to ride to the store with him. I kindly said, "No, that's all right. You go. I'll wait right here until you get back."

Sure enough, he started the 1959 General Motors Buick car up. He drove slowly down the dirt road. We had gotten a little gravel on the road now. Therefore, this helped with the dust from flying. I was jogging behind the car. We were about fifteen years old then. He was doing real fine. I thought to myself, "Okay so far."

When he got to the highway, he wanted me to be the lookout person for any cars coming before he entered the highway. You see, when you come off the dirt road and before entering the highway, there is a hill. So I go to the highway, and I gave him the okay after the traffic was clear.

I stayed on side of the highway while Cody drove the car to the store. It was late that evening. I knew it was getting close to time for Daddy to come back because Mr. N.T. was not going to drive home in the dark from our house.

I am not all sure if his truck headlights were working. Cody got on the highway headed to the store. He was in the middle of the highway, straddling the yellow line. I was so nervous. I was thinking what if a car came on the opposite side and hit him because he was taking up so much room on the highway. I know he had to be nervous too or he just can't drive.

When he topped that first hill past the church off to the right, he straightened the car up. He got on his side of the road. Everything went through my mind. What if Daddy comes back? What if he asks me what was I doing down at the highway? What if he asked me where was Cody? Better yet, what if Cody wrecks Daddy's car? What in the world was I going to tell him?

It seemed as though everything went through my mind. I walked back and forth. Well, after carefully thinking and asking myself all those questions and wearing out my shoes, I finally came to a conclusion. No pressure at all would have to be given. I finally knew what the answer would be. I knew it had to be my brother, me, or, my daddy. So I decided I was going to say, "Daddy, Cody stole your car and gone to the store, and I didn't have anything to do with it.

After sweating and carefully thinking out what I was going to say, Cody finally topped the hill coming back. I was impressed and proud of my brother until he made that right turn off the highway back onto the dirt road. He missed the whole dirt road. He tore all of the grass and dirt up on the side of it.

He got his honey bun and parked the car back at home. Daddy came not long after that. Daddy said, "Boy, I wonder who tore the side of that road up like that. I wonder did Press (Aunt Lil's husband short for Preston) run off that road like that." Since Daddy didn't question me, I didn't have to say anything. You see, there is no such thing as cracking under pressure with Daddy. All he had to do was look at you. When Daddy speaks, even the wild animals listen.

I look back to when we were working in the fields. Cody and I were foolish or it was just plain old amazing. The three of us had worked in the fields in the morning. It was time for our dinner break. Cody and I played basketball behind the house after dinner time. We felt dog tired after playing. This suited daddy because he was watching his favorite shows on television. As soon as we flopped into the chairs daddy would get up and say well it's time to go back to the field. You would think Cody and I would have learned to rest instead of playing ball. But we didn't we did it every time.

One late hot afternoon while the three of us were in the field picking cotton, daddy says y'all keep picking. I need to go to town to the doctor. He told us that he think he might have had a stroke. He told us to keep working.

Of course, it was difficult to work and do nothing to help our daddy. The stroke had affected his right side. But he insisted on driving himself to the doctor using his left foot on the gas pedal and brakes. Cody offered to drive daddy to the doctor, but he would not hear of it. I guess he was afraid of Cody going into town with no driver's license. I was a witness that he could drive.

Daddy was telling us later that he was losing the feeling in his whole right side. He improved after that episode.

During this school year there was a young man in upper class that was in the service at the same time as my brother. Everyone tried to support our fellow students when they were away serving our country. I wrote letters to my brother as well as Sonny. He wrote me as he did many other friends at the school. He was pretty popular among the school students. It was always a meeting in the cafeteria on Fridays or every other Friday mornings. All kinds of announcements were made during that time. This particular morning it was a special announcement made. I heard through the grape vine that a couple of students were upset and crying. But I did not know the reason for the upset. I sat down about middle ways of the cafeteria and the second seat from the end of the table

The room was quiet. The announcement came. Sonny had been killed. Everyone was in shock. I was in complete shock. I had just gotten a letter from him a couple of weeks before. The school had prayer and tried to encourage everyone to stay calm. Most were in disbelief. His body was shipped back home.

Before his body was ready for viewing I walked to the mailbox to get the mail. The old dusty road with a little gravel to the highway was always an enjoyable walk. You have time to think and enjoy some peace. I had written my brother to let him know about the death of Sonny. When I opened the mailbox I pulled out a letter with a military address on it. I knew it was too soon to get a return letter from my brother because I had only mailed his letter three days prior to going to the mailbox. But I thought it was probably a letter from him since Sonny was shipped home and he probably had the news already. Instead it was a letter from Sonny. I almost fainted. My heart sank. Apparently he had written me this letter and mailed it right before his death.

This is when I confided in my teacher Miss Ross. I told her about the letter. I went on to tell her that I had loss my mom a year before. And how it was just my dad and I home along with

Cody. She was very encouraging. I was grateful that she was a friend and a good listener.

Even with the tragedy this year was a pretty good year. Having my friends and having fun with them made all the difference. I recall that year a table full of girls including myself had gotten into some trouble talking in the library. Mrs. Polk was our Librarian. You could hear a pin drop when she was there. She would call your name out loud if you were talking and sometimes embarrassing you.

The reason all six girls had gotten into trouble was because of a friend with an idea. We were whispering. It wasn't even the whispering that got us into trouble in the first place. It was when one person whispered, if you had a chance to change your race which race would you want to be changed to and you cannot be your own race? One person said Chinese, one person said Hawaiian, and we reached our good friend Joanne. Apparently, she had her mind made up and hoping no one picked her choice when it came around to her. Joanne says; I want to be-you know-you know-what you call the race-you know what I'm talking about-that's it Puerto-Rican! She did not pronounce her choice correctly. While pronouncing her choice incorrectly this caused the whole table to have an outburst of laughter.

Thank goodness for the bell so we could leave the room. Big trouble we would have been in with Mrs. Polk. By the end of my tenth grade year I learned that the schools in the area were being integrated. I began to feel sad. I had to leave the school and my friends. I was going to be attending Middleton High.

I spent the summer in Michigan thinking about the new school in the fall. My sister Idell made sure I had nice clothes for the upcoming year. Upon returning back to Bolivar and the farm, I was bracing myself for what was to come. I did not know what to expect. The thinking about it before was more of a worry than actually attending. My nerves were all over the place.

In visiting my sisters and brothers in Detroit, I was able to stay busy. I spent time with friends that I had made through my previous visits during the summer months. The places in Detroit were much more fun than what we had back in the country. It is a very busy place compared to Bolivar.

Regina and I spent time with a few of her friends. She had her driver's license now. Idell gave her the opportunity to drive us around. The old Ford Galaxy would go two feet backwards before it went forward after putting it in drive. Regina kept driving it anyway.

I recall one night she and I stopped at a gas station for gas. Regina says "I need to get some gas before we get home. How much money do you have?" I replied; "I do not have any." She pulled into the gas station. With the windows down she was discussing the total amount of gas to get with the money she had. The young gas attendant asked; "how much?" She went over the amount once more. As Regina counted her change, the gas attendant was listening. He began to pump. Regina says to the attendant just give me a dollar's worth of gas. Well apparently the attendant thought for some reason she had more than a dollar. He ended up giving her two dollars' worth of gas. It was enough to get us home since we were just around the corner from home.

I was having fun this summer watching the fireworks. We had firecrackers back home but, I had never seen the fireworks before. The boat rides and amusement parks were great! I had always thought it was something special to have a truck come down the street and bring you ice cream to purchase. We always made our homemade ice cream or drove ten miles to get an ice cream cone in town.

Once I arrived back home in Bolivar I was bracing myself for my new school. I recall discussing the school we were to attend with my cousin Ruthie and Cody. I laid out my new clothes the night before. The next morning I picked up my pen, pencil, notebook, and my nerves and headed down the road on my journey to my new school with Cody and Ruthie.

Middleton High School

Starting my eleventh grade in the fall, I was bussed to Middleton High School six miles away. The first school building was built in 1873. The years between 1929 and 1940 several school consolidated with the school. In 1968 the school was integrated. Middleton high was known as the home of the Tigers. The principal at the time was Mr. Carroll. We were nervous at the beginning. The students who were already there were a little uneasy themselves. Some were more acceptable than others. This was the very first year that African Americans and whites came together as a student body.

The first day Cody, Ruthie and I waited for the bus. Ruthie was in her senior year. The lady bus driver was nice. We always sat on the seat with each other when possible. Whites pretty much stayed to themselves and so did the hand full of African Americans.

Each morning I would get up and cook breakfast and walk to the highway and wait for the school bus. The night before consisted of working in the fields, making dinner and doing my homework. There were nights I was almost too sleepy to finish my homework. And each day I was met with some challenges that I had to overcome.

When I walked down the hall, the white boys would be standing in the halls. When they saw me coming one may push his friend in front of me. This caused me to bump him. If they thought they were being funny, they weren't. If they were trying to be friendly, they were going about it the wrong way. A simple hello would have broken the ice on the communication between us. This one particular day, one boy was pushed into me. I thought enough is enough. I pushed back, and the principal saw me.

I was called to the office. And I was talked to by him. He stated that they had to get used to us and we had to get used to them.

We were interrupted by a telephone call. He had to take the call. I waited outside his office. There was a female senior who took a typing class with me. She said with a nice southern accent, "Mable what are you doing in here?" I told her about what happened.

She said, "I saw the whole thing." The principal overheard the conversation. So he let me go back to class. Thank god for that nice senior!

A few evenings later Cody, Daddy, and I were watching television when the telephone rang. I answered the telephone with "hello!" A voice on the other end says, "Hello Mable!" "This is Kate." With her nice southern accent she went on to tell me she and I shared some classes together.

In the conversation she says to me, "Whatever you do, do not tell my momma I called you. She would just skin me alive." She called a few more times.

During the year of 1968, things were discussed, and some things were not heard of discussing. There were relatives of a different race but we could not talk about it openly. It wasn't that we couldn't share, no one wanted to mention it. Plus, the white students did not want to do so openly in fear that his or her fellow classmates knew that they had an African American as a relative.

Around the second time she called, Cody asked, "Who was that on the telephone?" I told him it was Kate. Daddy moved to the edge of his seat and leaned forward. His words were "Who did you say that was? And do you know who that is?" I mentioned that she was just a girl in my class. Daddy said, "That's your cousin, but you can't go to school and talk about it."

Well, I did not go to school and talk about it. Kate and I graduated together. She never spoke a word, and I did not speak a word about it. We had some ways alike, "crazy"! A better way to put it is that we liked to have fun. She was related to me on my Daddy's side of the family. I kept this secret and kept the peace. I respected her privacy then and I respect it now. I went through school thinking nothing of it. I did not get an attitude or felt bad about it. My dad says "don't talk about it." Therefore I did not. I have learned in life that the best recipe for a bad attitude is to just have a good attitude.

Here is another secret. Or was it really a secret? It was extremely hot one summer day. It was dry and daddy wanted it to rain for the crops. Daddy purchased me, Cody, and himself an orange crush pop. Now, Cody and I drank our pop up right away. Daddy sat his pop in the refrigerator. I guess he must have had it in there for about three days.

Every day at midday, Cody would go open the refrigerator. He would say Daddy hadn't drunk his pop yet. The second day, he would go back to the refrigerator. And he would watch that pop. What Cody did not know was that he was watching Daddy's pop in the middle of the day to see if Daddy had drank his pop. And Daddy was watching it in the evening to see if anybody had drunk his pop. Talk about torcher! The sweat was beginning to build.

Well, on the third day, Cody could not take it any longer. I guess he figured he had been tortured enough. Cody took the pop bottle opener, and carefully went around all sides of the cap. This was so that the cap did not bend. He took two or three swallows out of the bottle. He put some water in the bottle to replace the pop he had taken. He carefully put the cap back on by tapping it into place and carefully making sure all sides were even.

Daddy came in that very evening. He went to the refrigerator. He got the pop out this time. Cody and I were watching television. Daddy came out with the pop. Cody and I looked at each other.

Daddy sat in his recliner chair with the pop in his hand. As he was sitting down, he said nothing. He made his usual long tired sound Whew! He looked over at Cody and made one statement, "Somebody drank out of my pop!" We never looked up and did not say a word. Since Daddy didn't ask a question, we did not have a comment. But you just could not pull any wool over Momma or Daddy's head.

One fall morning, I did not get out of bed. It was a school morning. I had stomach cramps. It was more painful than usual this particular morning.

Daddy came to my bedroom door. He asked, "Aren't you going to school?" I told him my stomach was hurting.

He went into the kitchen. He boiled some water. He poured the water into a mason canning jar and put the top on it tight. He wrapped a cloth around it, brought it to my bedside, and told me, "Put this to your stomach; it might help you."

He looked a little lost. I guess because this is something Momma would be doing. She was there to take care of all the other girls. Daddy did the best he knew how. This was the gentle but loving side of him.

This year we had to do a school project. I chose to do my bedroom as my project. I told Daddy about it. I tore all the wallpaper off the wall. Daddy went to town and purchased the sheet rock (dry wall) and plaster. He helped me with the project with measurements and nails. I painted the room a light green. This was a time I saw my Daddy proud. I got an A on the project. It was a good feeling to have my dad helping me with the heavy part of the project.

By the time I felt good about one thing something else came along. Our school played basketball against my formal school one night. My cousin and I attended that game. When we walked into the gym, we weren't comfortable in where to sit. I followed my cousin. We sat on the side with our formal school. We discussed who to cheer for but did not know which after discussing it. This was our first year at the new school. We ended up cheering for both mostly under our breath. Talk about between a rock and a hard place. We did not want to split the support for the schools. The old school lost the game by a couple of points.

The next morning, as I stepped off the bus, I was greeted by the principal's wife. The first thing came out of her mouth was "I have a bone to pick with you, young lady." I do not recall if anything was said or what was said exactly between us after that. But what she failed to realize was that we could have supported our school had we had more support as students from our classmates or the school as a whole. That night would have been a little more comfortable, and our longtime friends from Bolivar would have understood.

The teacher in this school I admired was my English teacher. She was rather quiet and nice. She kept us on our toes with her pop quizzes. Therefore you had to always read. You did not have much choice when it came to learning. You had to either learn the work or failed the class.

I enjoyed the Home Economic class. It was very interesting. We had to make our own outfit and model it on stage. The modeling took place at night at the school. It was a lot of fun.

In the twelfth grade, things eased up some; I thought. When it was time to take our graduation pictures, our fitting for pictures came as no surprise. All the white girls put on their outfits first and had their pictures taken. Then the four female African American students put on the outfits last to have their pictures taken.

When the time came for the prom, I did not attend the one at my old school, which I was invited to by an old classmate. I did not go to the banquet that my school had. Somehow, with everything happening around me, it took away my desire to be involved.

I think back to my twelfth grade year

When I had taken one of our finals in our Home Economics class, on a particular test, I had the highest grade. When another student asked in front of the class who got the highest grade, the teacher motioned her head in my direction. I was acknowledged.

It was without verbally mentioning my name. Did this bother me? Of course it did. I made the honor roll my last year in Middleton High. Even though I did not go to the Banquet I was so very proud of myself and happy to be finishing. I knew once I made it, all I had to do was to look forward to the future and not look back.

I am kind of glad I graduated from Middleton High. It was an experience I will never forget. I met some good kind hearted teachers and students. I learned that you certainly cannot judge everyone the same. I truly believe the experience and the change were good for everyone. With my struggles growing up and the two years I spent at this school made me a stronger and better person. I felt it was getting me prepared for the world. My growing up country and heading for a bigger world, I needed some tough things I guess to teach me how to cope with any future struggles. I knew there would probably be more experiences and struggles like this. I found strength through those struggles. Therefore, any struggles that came my way I was going to try to overcome and continue holding on to the strength beyond strength.

The schools and the community are even more diversified now. The whole town has changed and continuing to grow. The good old friendly southern hospitality remains. It is good to see that everyone pulled together to help one another. The police department in Bolivar and Middleton are much larger. I guess you have heard the expression what a difference a day makes.

When I graduated my twelfth grade year, I followed suit. I moved to Detroit in hopes of a better opportunity. There were some hard times. But there were some tender loving times. I was able to see these things while Momma and Daddy were living. They were respected, and they respected others.

Cody continued to live with daddy. He could have given up after I graduated high school and left Daddy. But he did not. Daddy loved and treated him like a son instead of a grandson.

Daddy was getting older now, and I had to move on. It wasn't easy leaving him, especially knowing he was not very well. The good thing was Cody was there to help him.

Daddy still sold eggs just like his father did when he was living. I remember Cody writing me a letter. In this letter, he wrote, "Will you please mail me just one egg? Daddy has sold all we've had." Daddy got to the place he could not farm anymore; this came after Cody graduated the following year. By this time, his income, I guess, came from social security, and he was the only one he had to feed.

After getting to Michigan I worked and attended school. Later I married my husband and to this union three children were born.

After settling down in my marriage with two children at the time, I remember getting a telephone call letting me know that Daddy had a stroke. He was living alone. Daddy was coming from the barn. And he felt light headed and dizzy. So he thought he would lie down under the brush near the house in the shade for a minute but realized later he could not get up.

He was supposed to be meeting his friend, Mr. Booker, down at Mt. Olive Church to do some work. Mr. Booker called the house with no answer. Mr. Booker told me that he knew something wasn't right because when Daddy gives his word on something, he keeps it. This is what made him go check up on him.

As he drove up the road and approaching the house, there, he found Daddy on the ground. He entered our house and called Daddy's brother Ola and for the ambulance. They took him to Jackson General Hospital. He had indeed had a stroke.

This is what my dad meant. "Your word is your bond." Had he been a liar, not dependable and untrustworthy, Mr. Booker probably would not have come. There, Daddy would have been in the country, ten miles from town, without help.

All of Daddy's children lived in another state at the time of his illness. Daddy was in Jackson General Hospital. The stroke paralyzed his right side. He complained of having a headache. He asked for ben-gay medicated cream. In his mind this cream would help if applied on his temple. He was treated and later released.

After being released from the hospital, Daddy ended up in a nursing home in Milan, Tennessee. His elder brother Ola was very good and protective over Daddy. He showed all the love and concern any brother could have given. It is good to have family that cares. I am grateful to Uncle Ola and to his children!

As I think back, when Freddie, Carl, and James went home around Thanksgiving for their usual winter hunting, I rode with them. We visited Daddy at the nursing home. Uncle Ola would get upset and worried when Daddy would not know him on some of his visits. Daddy would have seizures after his stroke. This was something common in some stroke victims.

I must tell you. When I walked into Daddy's room at the nursing home, I was surprised! There was my big, strong, once-hardworking Daddy, lying there with a feeding tube in his nose. He had lost so much weight, and his beautiful white hair was longer than he would ever have worn it.

He was awake as we walked into his room. The first thing he said was "I want some salmon and rice." I went to the nurse's station and asked for the doctor. The nurse called him. I asked the doctor, "If we wanted to have Daddy moved, could we?"

The doctor told me that he did not see any reason that he could not be moved. He also asked what my plans were. I told him I would like to get him to Detroit. He gave me his telephone number to his home. He told me to let him know what we decide to do. And he would be glad to help on his end.

Upon my return visit with Daddy the next day, I walked to the foot of Daddy's bed so he could see me. I asked, "Daddy, would you like to go back to Detroit with us?" He raised his head. He replied, "Baby, I'll go anyway you want me to." I knew he had to be missing family and home.

When I went home (to Daddy's house) that night, I made telephone calls. I contacted Clinora in Detroit. She contacted Regina. Regina worked for the Delta Airlines at the time and set up Daddy and Carl's flight. Clinora looked for a nursing home in Detroit. I called my doctor's office and set up an address for Daddy to have.

Daddy's doctor said he had to have a contact person and a mailing address. With permission from my doctor, it was all set in place. Carl stayed and rode the airplane to Detroit with Daddy.

Once Daddy got into the nursing home, we all played a part in helping him. I recall when Ethel and I went to visit him. Daddy had a seizure while we were there. We had never witnessed him having a seizure before. After the seizure, he would be totally out of it. Ethel tried to do CPR on Daddy, and I ran to get the nurse. This must have been what Uncle Ola had seen when he visited daddy.

When Allie visited, she fed him. And my sister-in-law Lorene would massage him until he fell asleep. I recall not being satisfied with his body not being clean. I asked, "Daddy, do you mind if I wash you?" His reply: "Go to it!" And he told me how to do it.

After a complete body wash, brushing his hair, and oiling him up, he said, "Show feels good." I stood back and looked at him as he fell asleep. My mind went back to when he would let me cut his hair on the front porch when I was about fifteen or sixteen years old. He had the most beautiful white hair.

Daddy never remarried, even though Momma wanted him to. My dad did not date right away. It took a long time. He was more concern about what his children thought.

He started liking one lady later on. She was a little younger. He told my brother that he had a dream. In this dream our mom kept blocking him as he tried to leave out of the door. He figured momma was telling him don't go, this is not the person for you. Even though he went to visit this lady a few times, he stopped a little while after that dream.

It was then he started receiving these telephone calls from a widow lady Ms. "O". Her husband had been deceased for some years. At the time daddy was unaware of who she was. Ms. "O" later told me that he would hang up on her when she called him on the telephone. She said, "Well I just kept calling." Personally I am so glad she did. Daddy visited Ms. "O". They became good friends.

Whenever he visited her he had good meals and companion. She did not drive therefore, Daddy would take her shopping and to visit her daughter in Mississippi. They made quite a pair.

In my conversations with her, she told me many times how my dad told her that if something should ever happen to him that his children would continue to call and visit her. She seemed so happy that it came true. Her last hospital admission I visited her. She was sent home as a hospice patient. Upon her death, I helped the nurse clean her up for her body to be transported.

When children lose one of their parents, they sometimes forget about how the parent left behind feels. Children have their lives, and the surviving parent should have a life also. It is not that they have forgotten the deceased parent at all. They become even lonelier.

I worked in a senior care living place. I have watched the seniors who are lonely. Their spouses passed away, and they feel as if no one cares. Their children work and have their personal life. And they are left feeling with emptiness in their own life, even though they do not want to interfere with their children's lives.

I have actually seen children who want their parent to have someone but are protective over their well-being. You have seniors who are ill. Yes, they can sometimes carry on like teenagers. They fall in love like anyone else.

In Daddy's case, he still lived in our home at the time, and his lady friend still lived in hers. He looked forward to seeing her, and she looked forward to seeing him. The good part in this is that they brought each other happiness. This type of happiness, children could not possibly bring.

This is when not having selfish love comes in. I knew that I wanted to have someone in my life and to be able to love and be loved by a companion. Would it have been fair for me to want all this in my life and be selfish and not want my dad to have the same thing?

Daddy lived until he was seventy-three years old. And his lady friend lived on until she was one hundred and five years old.

CLASS REUNION

A FEW YEARS AGO, WE had a class reunion at the old school I transferred from. I say "we" because they have always made me feel a part of their class, even though I graduated from another school. Not that some students at my school weren't nice.

I remember when some of my formal classmates wanted to have another reunion; they asked me if I would head it. It took me a while to say yes simply because I wasn't sure how the rest of the classmates felt.

After I agreed, I called my friend, a former classmate Sandra who now lives in North Carolina. I asked her if she would rather head it since she had graduated from Bolivar Industrial. She kindly said, "No! But I'll help you." She and I put on this class reunion in Bolivar from Michigan and North Carolina.

I did not feel comfortable coming myself, so I included every student who was our grade, our age, and who had attended Bolivar Industrial High School to this reunion. They were forced to attend other schools as well as I had to. I did not exclude anyone. We had teachers honored because without them we would not be where we are today. We gave our retired teacher, my old algebra teacher, Mr. Boone the opportunity to cater our dinner since he was now in the business. Mr. Boyd my eighth grade teacher was most helpful with some of the student contacts. He was also very supportive at the reunion.

Classmates who still lived in the areas of Bolivar gave their 110 percent. They called me and wanted to know how they could help. I certainly appreciated the support. I felt, at that moment, that we were like family.

There were classmates who came who had never been to a class reunion. There were friends that I had not seen since tenth grade. Unfortunately, I have never attended a class reunion at the school I graduated from. My goal is to do so soon. Now that I am married and with children, my directions in life have changed.

I visited Miss Lake. She was now known as Mrs. McKinney. I, along with some other students, presented her with an award. Her health was failing at the time of our visit. We sang the school song with her. She remembered every word. As we were leaving her home we could still hear her singing the school song. The same students and I went on to visit our Physical Education teacher, Miss Ross in the next town and presented an award to her as well. She was now known as Mrs. Murphy. As we were leaving she walked us to the van. We said our goodbyes. I mentioned to her maybe you should go back into the house. She replied, "I like watching people when they drive away." As I pulled off my memories went back to when she was such a mentor to me in school during the time I needed it most. She stood there in the driveway as I looked through my review and side mirrors. How can we forget people that have helped us in our lives?

My mom and dad always taught us to help others. Always try to give back to the same people that have helped you along the way. Even though we as students disagreed with our teachers while we were in school, we knew they were trying to look out for our best interest. And to simply put it, they said learn, stay out of trouble, and be respectful. I've never forgotten my principals and teachers. I am indeed thankful for their guidance and tough love. This goes also for our parents and grandparents.

With the loss of four brothers, a sister, and young nieces and nephews, my direction and focus changed here lately. It was the curiosity about our heritage that brought some questions from our younger generations in the family. So I decided to get interviews from older relatives and do some further research.

I want to tell them that it was not easy. There were struggles and obstacles in the way, but it did not stop the journey I was on.

If grandparents, parents, and I made it, they can too. This goes for anyone that set a goal and works at it.

Some of the information I collected were of several interviews from family members. Some were from old stories and history. Our history speaks of the plantations, which is a large agricultural estate where slave farm hands worked the crops. A planter is a person that owned a plantation and the property of slaves. The crops consisted of cotton, corn, sugar, tobacco, cane and timber. The southern states were well known for plantations and having crops.

During the plantation period the slave owner's practiced the influence of reproduction of slaves. This was so they could increase their wealth. They encouraged sexual relations of the female and male slaves for babies to be born. There were sexual relations between the slave owners with the aim to produce more slave children. This was done in order to save money so they did not have to purchase other slaves. Look at the money that was continued to be made off a woman that had to have children for the convenience of someone else. This meant he watched his children become a slave and worked like a slave. At that time slave children were disowned by their slave owner which was their parent.

The field hands were somewhat called lower class. They picked, tobacco, pulled corn, cut timber, and whatever else was needed to be done. The higher class was pretty much the house slaves, the servants in the house working as cooks, housekeepers, and baby sitters. They all were considered slaves. None of the positions were easy.

Even if you did not do hard labor in the fields from sun up to sun down, your pride and self-esteem took some hardships. I often wonder if for one year, the slaves and their masters had traded places, would it have taken years for the slaves to be freed. We, as African Americans, sometimes forget the struggles that our ancestors have gone through. It seems as though today our young generation are taking life and freedom for granted. They are not realizing that their ancestors lived on a plantation wishing and fighting for freedom. Our young generations do not want to experience what their ancestors experienced.

Since I lived in Tennessee and had gone to school there, I thought I would take a tour of a place I had not visited before in the area. I heard about the Ames Plantation through family members a couple of years ago.

My family and I took a tour of the Ames Plantation in Tennessee. The Ames Plantation is located on Ames Drive in Grand Junction. We could see work being done as we toured in late August 2012.

As we made the turn onto the roads of the Ames Plantation, it took me back to the memories of the corn fields and cotton fields where we use to work hard to make a living. When I came along, chopping cotton was about two dollars per day under the hot sun. This was from sun up to sun down.

Some days were hotter than others. We would collect water from the well and the springs. The water was then put into a fruit jar and taken to the fields. We would share the water from this fruit jar. There were times we packed lunches.

Cotton chopping and picking salaries were much less when my older siblings came along. It was even less with the slaves. Think of what the slaves had to endure to keep a roof over their heads in order to feed their families.

On the Ames Plantation, you couldn't help but put yourself in the place of those slaves. The one-room houses were for everyone in their families. As you walked in the one-room house, it felt like a large box. One house still had the old wooden weaving board, three baskets of cotton, and a fire place. I can image this was for display only for people that were touring the place. The larger houses were apparently for the larger families.

It is my understanding that the Old Jones Chapel MB Church was rebuilt or remodeled. Also, the long, red building was apparently a building where the horses used to be fed and rested.

You will see the upcoming pictures of the small housing and the school for children to learn. There is an old cemetery located on the land. You could see the cows, and corn fields. The thought of the sweat and hard work these slaves had to endure. I am pretty sure no one in their right mind would want to experience such a task.

Before reaching the plantation, I asked my husband to stop the van. I wanted our grandchildren to get out and pick a bow or two of cotton in a roadside cotton field so they can get a feel of what they were about to learn of the slaves working day and how they lived. This was to set the stage for what they were about to see. They had a chance to see the large fields and long rows. By it being in the month of a hot August day, this gave them an opportunity to feel the heat and understand the labor. They were told stories about slavery. I explained to them how their grandparents and great grandparents had to live and do without a lot of things.

We can read and hear stories all day long. But, when you have lived the way the slaves had to live, the story will have a different meaning. Why? Until you have lived it, you cannot begin to know the feeling. It is the same as having a baby. You can see the labor. You can imagine the labor. Until you have gone through the labor, it is then you will know for sure the experience.

Slaves Picking Cotton

The slaves had to pick cotton, bow by bow, stalk by stalk, row by row, until the fields were completed. It took a whole lot of prayer and patience in those days. Even today, it still takes prayer and patience. It also takes the willingness to put all things into place.

The slaves were beaten and forced to work in the fields. They were denied education and burned out of their homes. As you will see in some of the pictures, some of the living quarters were very small.

Now, we have the opportunity to go to work without being forced and physically abused. We have choices now to educate ourselves and have better jobs. We should take advantage of it. No one can take your knowledge. We may be good at sports, but as I once heard, don't let your big feet take you where your head can't keep you. In other words, you can put yourself in those shoes, but take some knowledge and education with you in your head. When your body is all broken up and the money is gone, what do you really have?

Take a good look at your forefather's history and continue to educate and work for a better tomorrow. And encourage this to your children. Refuse to be taken back. Standing on the corners, robbing and stealing, and selling drugs is not the way.

To all young generations whatever you do stay out of the drug house so you will not have to go to the court house and end up in the jail house. Working and educating yourself and your children are the paths to take.

God made up our generation of many races. It is my understanding that Grandpa West was made up of Cherokee Indian. According to Clinora, checking the censors, Caroline, his mother, was of some Irish descent. I think about how God has given each of us our own personality, attitudes, and beauty. What he gave us was a chance in life to display our behavior and the will to better ourselves and to help others as our grandparents did.

It is by our own choosing to carry ourselves in a respectable and fashionable manner. He has given us all our needs to continue what he has taught us in the Bible. When we step out in this world, remember we are not only representing the way of my great-great grandpa Charles but that of our parents, spouses, children, and that of God.

We are not perfect in this world. Mistakes are made throughout the lives of all of Gods' children. It is what we have learned from our mistakes that can and will make a difference in our lives and the lives of others. We should keep in mind what the slaves must have gone through.

History on the Ames Manor House was constructed in 1847 by Mr. John Jones. I recently learned from the touring brochures and from the Center Director Dr. Rick Carlisle the following information about the Ames Plantation on Tuesday, July 23, 2013 at 9:50PM, he quotes; "Ames plantation is privately owned and operated by the Successor Trustees of the Hobart Ames Foundation and operates for the benefit of the University of Tennessee. The Ames Plantation is one of 10.

Research and Education Centers within the Agricultural Experiment Station System. The Ames Plantation is the largest single land resource base that UT AgResearch has access too. The Ames Plantation is 18,400 acres in size and maintains the 3rd oldest Aberdeen Angus Beef Cattle Herd in the nation and provides the grounds and the administrative support for conducting the National Championship for Field Trailing Bird Dogs and has since 1915. The Ames Plantation raises approximately 2,500 acres of corn, cotton, soybeans, wheat and grain sorghum and maintains 12,000 acres of mixed hardwoods and pine timber. Ames Plantation superimposes agricultural research projects on all aspects of the row crop and livestock commodities as well as the forestry/wildlife program. While being privately owned, we do conduct research for several major universities in the southern U.S. as well as the University of Tennessee".

In our telephone conversation on Monday, July 22, 2013, Dr. Carlisle says touring is available with twenty or more people. The requirements consist of a one month advance notice.

I would like to share some stories with you about a couple of cemeteries in the Bolivar and Grand Junction areas. The LaGrange cemetery had 160 confederate soldiers with marked graves. On small pieces of wood were the soldier's initials. The wood was somehow destroyed later. It was most likely used for firewood during the bitter cold weather in the year of 1863-1864. This cemetery remains in the community and maintained by the LaGrange Cemetery Association.

If we studied our history in school, we would have learned that while there were struggles for the slaves, they found strength with the help of Ulysses S. Grant and John Eaton. The year of 1862 in the fall, they were on their way to Vicksburg. Grant and his troops were delayed in Grand Junction, Tennessee. It is my understanding that there were thousands of refugee slaves. The slaves begged for protection. Grant directed Eaton to form a camp for the slaves on the corn and cotton plantation that were abandoned.

The plantation owners had left therefore the African-Americans were hired. They were supervised to work. The former slaves were paid to work and cut wood for the union steamers. The slaves were later enlisted in the Union Army. With the sales from the crops and military wages they were able to get their basic needs.

History also lies in Bolivar, Tennessee with the Polk Cemetery. This cemetery was established by an uncle of our United States President James K. Polk. His family is buried in this cemetery.

History is amazing and very interesting. It is something everyone should learn. It tells us that residents in West Tennessee were faced with neglected fields and failing industries. The freedmen move north or to the cities in search of work. They made careers in iron and steel railroads and domestic work. The farmers were forced to start over and the freedmen that stayed were hired by the land owners to sharecrop the land. They worked the land in exchange for a place to live.

They saw little or no money for their hard work from early morning to late evening labor. In late 1935 there were 63 percent of West Tennessee farmers that became tenants. While the slaves did not escape, they continued to work. They were indebted to everyone.

I was too young to vote when President John Kennedy and Richard Nixon were running for president leading up to the 60s. It became a challenge for African Americans. During this time, the white residents tried to keep African-Americans from voting.

During the winter months there were hundreds of African American tenant farmers that were evicted from white owner's farms. This was just after the harvest and during the bitter cold. There were tents that were set up for shelter for the winter.

I also found out that in 1959, the Fayette County Democratic Executive Committee was charged with failing to let African Americans vote in the democratic primary. This was the first federal lawsuit brought under the 1957 Civil Rights Act.

Tennessee has produced many famous actors, singers, and writers. Alex Haley, a writer, wrote "Roots." There was also a movie made. He is buried in the Savannah Cemetery where his grandparents, Alex and Queen Haley, are buried. On the Tennessee River Trail, you'll be able to visit his grandparent's grave site as well.

I also learned buried in this cemetery is Mary Elizabeth Patterson. She is known for playing in *I Love Lucy* as Little Rick's babysitter, Mrs. Matida Trumbalk. And the first made movie, *Walking Tall*, was made in Tennessee.

There were and are many country, blues, rock and roll, and gospel music and famous singers were originated in the state of Tennessee.

While I lived in the Hardeman county area I was so anxious to move out of the country setting for a chance for a better opportunity in the North. It seems as though I followed the footsteps of my slave ancestors. I learned about history in school, but it is more interesting now. I thought I had it hard growing up. My growing up does not compare to the way the slaves lived.

Look how far the African-Americans have come. Slaves struggled for survival in the state of Tennessee. Here in 2013, their ancestors are holding high positions in the work environment throughout the country and the world. In Dr. Carlisle's email, he states that slavery is a part of history that no one can deny. He went on to say; he agrees that the more we can publicize this portion of our history, the less likely it is to ever happen again.

Upon my visit to the plantation without knowing all the history I could feel history. I closed my eyes for a moment trying to imagine what it must have been like during such a difficult time in slavery. My eyes watered as I walked the grounds, especially when I stepped inside the one room housing unit. This was history and a history I had to accept.

The following pictures were taken on my visit to the Plantation. Please see pictures on the next few pages of the plantation in Tennessee (Try to put you in that environment) The Ames plantation was a very clean area.

Entrance to the Ames Plantation

There is a fireplace located on the opposite side of this one room house.

Appears to be an old weaving board

Little red school house located left of house

Refurbished school at the plantation

The National Bird Field Trail
Championship for Bird Dogs
1896-1996

Old Jones Chapel MB Church

Slavery began many years ago. There were many different slaves. This did not only include African Americans and Indians in the state of Tennessee. This goes back to the Greek and Roman times. Slavery is the special sanctioning of involuntary servitude imposed by one person or group upon another.

During slavery in the Ancient times, the slaves were formed to help build the Empires and for the economy. Their masters had children by their slaves. During that time the master could set their slaves free. But, the father of the children, their masters would make sure his children would not have a life of slavery.

I have heard that there was white slavery as well. It existed around the 17th century. There were slaves that worked hard under their masters that polished the master's silver, gold, and other labor. There were children born into slavery by their masters as well.

If my memory is correct, the state of Tennessee has a long Native American heritage. During the Bicentennial years the Cherokee Indians were the original Citizens in the state of Tennessee. There are many in the state of Tennessee that has Cherokees in their ancestry.

It is important to learn your history and heritage. The Cherokees were forced from their homes around the year of 1838. This forced them to travel to other areas in the U.S. Many lost their lives to the bitter cold winters. I had a chance to travel and visit the Smoky Mountains in Tennessee. It is a beautiful and educational place to visit.

During the historic time the Chickasaw Indians lived in northern Mississippi areas. Tennessee and Kentucky were used as hunting grounds. There is a Chickasaw State Park located in Henderson Tennessee. I can remember traveling there on a Bolivar Industrial School class trip one year. It is also a beautiful and educational place to visit.

In history I learned that there were some black slave owner's in 1830. They had possibly had some white ancestors. There were around three thousand or more such slaveholders in the south. They owned practically over twelve thousand slaves. There was the upper south and lower south. Between the two there were some economic differences of the free African Americans. One reason is because some of the slaveholders lived in the city and some in the country.

It was illegal to teach a slave to read or write. However, the children began to teach each other. Let us not forget the children played together.

There were legal sanctions over the African American population. All the slaves did not escape towards freedom. The slave owners attended church and did not allow the slaves at some point to have church services. When the slaves drove their masters to church, I believe they were allowed to sit in the balcony. With this happening the slaves gained knowledge. But as time moved forward, they were allowed to exercise their right to preach and teach. While their message would consist of their struggles, faith, and finding their strength in love for God, they were able to overcome what once stood as a road block and a closed door to becoming a clear path and an open door to some freedom.

Tensions began to rise. The church ministers were under pressure to preach about the policies taking place. It was when Abraham Lincoln won the 1860 election with no more new slave states that made the south break away the confederacy. This is when the Civil War began. Now it is my understanding that the war had killed slavery. This was supposed to have been before the thirteenth Amendment.

Several years after those struggles and prayers came some relief. The Thirteenth Amendment was passed by the senate around April of 1864. It passed the House of Representatives around January of 1865. It was approved along the lines of December, 1865. With three fourth of the states agreeing it made the rest of slaves free. It seems as though slavery existed in many races. Who determine which race had it worse? What matters is that slavery is slavery. It was forced upon people of many races. I ask myself; just how free are the slave ancestor's today? Struggles continue even in 2013.

Many years ago, when slave owners owned a slave, he was called the master. If the master died, in many cases, the slave was given or left in a will to his son, daughter, or other siblings. The slaves were inherited to someone in the family. It was my understanding that there were slaves that took on their master's name.

Some of the slaves did not want to leave after the master was deceased. I am sure they thought of where they would go or whose hand they would end up in. Some slaves were not listed by name making it difficult to locate in the censor reports. There was a fire many years ago which destroyed records. With time any headstones were either destroyed or faded from the weather over the years.

If each of us dig deep enough we may just find slavery in every race of people even outside of the United States.

Many of my ancestors are buried in Mt. Olive Cemetery, Mt. Zion Cemetery, both in Bolivar, Tennessee. Also, they are buried in Old Walnut Grove Cemetery, which is located in Hornsby, Tennessee.

Our roots have come farther than my great-great grandpa Charles. It has grown in multitudes. It took love, hope, faith, trust, courage, heartaches, determination, prayers, and perseverance to overcome the hardship of slavery.

There were anger, doubts, fears, and pain brought upon them. It took a higher being to bring our ancestors through from the past beyond the 1800s up to our today's society. We are indeed blessed. Many ancestors and siblings are gone but not forgotten.

Connecting our family tree and its roots, I felt a bond that I have never felt before. It was the learning and knowing of some of their history that made a difference. It was putting my feelings and thoughts back into their era and bondage. This made me think of the chain links to this generation.

Each generation struggled and suffered so that the next generation could have it better than the generation before. Each time, a family member fell from the tree another sibling came along. The losses did not stop the roots. The family tree continued to grow stronger. Education and the knowledge from the family roots will make us continue to learn.

It will still take determination, love, respect, faith, courage, hope, team work, and prayers to pull through this generation. We may not be in the same bondage that my grandparents and their parents and grandparents, but we are still climbing to have a better way to live in this society. There are still some heartaches, distrust, and lack of respect.

Just keep educating yourself. Knowledge is very important. Do not let all the suffering and the fight that your forefathers have gone through be wasted. Appreciate and learn from it! Make the struggles that you have endured better for the next generation. Someday your children will speak of these very things about history and their heritage. Collect as much information that you can so that you will be able to share with them your ancestor's struggles and strengths. What will you be able to tell them?

As slaves, and even after slavery, we were dared to do many things. The dares were what we set out to prove and overcome. Without coming out and telling you, you are still dared, even today.

- I dare you to pray.
- I dare you to be educated.
- I dare you to have determination and overcome hardships.
- I dare you to love one another.
- I dare you to recognize that you were freed.
- I dare you to respect yourself and others.
- I dare you to break the family tree chain of improvement.
- I dare you to let your skin color or race stand in your way with excuses.
- I dare you to get out of bondage.
- I dare you to overcome racism.
- I dare you to have hope.
- I dare you to have faith and trust in yourself and God.

• I dare you to move forward away from the auction block of slavery and possibly become the president of the United States of America. I dare you.

Before the 1800s books were kept rather poorly. Much had to do with the lack of communication and technology. Some were that African American people were treated less than humane.

Please keep in mind; it was slavery time for my grandparents and great grandparents. During slavery time, there was a lack of education. And they were not allowed to have the opportunity to attend schools the way we do today.

I'm sure many slaves were very smart. They may not have had all the education possible, but they were very intelligent. Our ancestors purchased land and churches. For example, my Grandpa West owned land.

As mentioned before, they were not allowed to have schools and to even have church services in some places. Please keep in mind that slaves were not freed until 1865. (Please search and read more on slavery). You will see in some stories of our siblings that education was hard to come by. They wanted the education. They just had a hard time trying to get it.

Back during that time, a lot of rapes took place. There were girls that were chased and raped on the way to and from school. This was not only of the African American race. When the women had babies by their rapist, they had no justice from it. I know this still applies today with women of all races. Many of the slave men had to stand by and accept what had happened to their loved ones. Babies were taken in by many African Americans that were of a mix race.

Many children were disowned by their rapist, even when they were aware that it was their child. God only knows what happened to the great-grandfathers and great-grandmothers during that time of all races.

In my interview with Aunt Lil some years before her death, I called her on the telephone one night. She gave me the following information in our conversation: Great grandpa Albert Sr. was six years old when he was put on an auction block and sold as a slave. He had come over on some type of boat. He was fourteen years old, and Violet was twelve years old when they jumped the broom (end of conversation).

Aunt Lil traveled and she tried to keep up on all the latest. She believed in family knowing family and the truth should be told. She would always say God didn't like ugly. I guess she had a point. If we deny loved ones, what nerve do we have to expect God not to deny us?

We did not have the pleasure of meeting my great grandparents. But there are family members who had the pleasure of meeting them and lived with Grandma Ollie.

I have learned that she was a midwife. She delivered babies throughout the community. She also delivered all of Momma's babies except the eldest and youngest brother, and the youngest child. I do not know the reason for my eldest brother not being delivered by her. Maybe grandma did not make it in time.

Grandma fell ill years later. My mom's sister Aunt Viola delivered my youngest brother. She attempted to deliver me, but I was in a breech position. Therefore, they sent for Dr. Lawrence who lived in town. It is my understanding that I was eventually born on a table that the doctor had brought with him. After some point, I was turned around. Daddy was even worried to the point that he told Momma; no more children Wesley B.

I am more than grateful that my momma pulled through this hard delivery. By giving birth to three children of my own, I know that giving birth to a child is not an easy task at all, even though it is a beautiful gift and a blessing.

Many years ago, there were a lot of childbirth deaths than today. Thank god for new technology. I can only think about how hard she had worked and that she already had given birth to twelve children prior to me. I, indeed, am blessed and thankful that God spared my momma. I guess Grandma Ollie would have sent for the doctor as well. I am just glad to be here writing this book, and my mother's life was spared.

Grandma Ollie was born in 1873. She married Grandpa West in 1899. It is my understanding that there was a girl according to the censors and my sources, that a four-year-old girl was present at the time of their marriage.

Grandma was a gardener. She grew many kinds of fruits and vegetables. She raised pigs and hundreds of chickens, guineas, turkeys, and geese using an incubator for hatching the eggs. She also made soap for washing clothes and the body. Her quilts and clothes were made by hand. She preserved the foods, marketed them, and sold many of her goods. She had one of the largest houses in the community.

According to my sisters, Grandma Ollie dropped corn bread dough off in the liquid of a pot of green vegetables leaving the dough white. Daddy was used to having his bread cooked until brown. The bread would be done, but Daddy hated when she did that. Sometimes, Grandma would be at the house when Momma was sick or when she had a baby. Of course, Daddy ate the bread. He did not have anything else. It was a blessing that Grandma Ollie was there to help. We had a family of thirteen. Look at how many times grandma had to come to help in our home. I am sure he appreciated all that grandma did for his family.

My dad's mom on other hand I heard was beautiful. She was stern and believed in your word being your bond. I was told by my elder sister that momma told her once a story about my dad and his mom. Momma and daddy were sitting down at the table eating. They kept hearing this noise. After trying to ignore the noise, they decided to get up to see what and where the noise was coming from. It was Grandma Anna. Daddy had borrowed her plow. He did not take it back after he borrowed it. There Grandma Anna was pulling the plow with her bare hands down the dirt road. Daddy kept telling her he was going to take the plow back. She continued pulling on the plow. Daddy had borrowed the plow and did not take it back at the time he promised he would. When she meant your word is your bond, she meant it.

COUSIN INTERVIEWS

I N MY TELEPHONE INTERVIEW with my cousin Minnie, she remembered Grandma Ollie very well. She described Grandma as a sweet and hardworking woman. She also was a good cook. She raised her own pig for when they had a big dinner at her son's (Tommie) church.

After Uncle Tommie became a minister, Grandma was happy. When they finally got the church built and he became pastor, Grandma Ollie shouted across the church pulpit. Minnie remembered her being so very proud and supportive of Uncle Tommie. Her favorite song was "Lord, get ready, you got to move."

When Uncle James (Grandma's youngest son) went away to the service, He sent her cactus plants by mail. She planted them all on the right side of her house. It is my understanding that Grandma had diabetes.

Back in the 1800s, during the civil war and the slaves were freed, I was told that Grandpa was three years old. This is when the war was ending. He remembered waving goodbye to his mother on the back of a wagon with some slaves on it.

According to Minnie, at that time, Mary Curry was sixteen years old. Mary was grandpa's half-sister. It was an African American couple there. The wife was ill, and the man took Grandpa and his sister in for Mary Curry to help care for his ill wife for a while.

Minnie remembers how she used to cook for Grandpa West. She says Grandpa did not like biscuits but loved his corn bread and his cheese According to Minnie he was the only African American man that could vote during this time. And he would get up early on voting day and walk along the highway in hopes that someone would give him a ride. End of interview.

This section shows an interview with my cousin Sandra. This is the daughter of Minnie and granddaughter of aunt Lil, sources consist of interviews and censor's report that she volunteered to submit to me.

According to Sandra, Aunt Mary Jones died in 1945 according to the censor's report. Mary first married William Bid Macon. She later married Jim Jones. Mary was considered an outside child, but her grandmother did not want to talk about that.

She went on to tell me that Grandpa John West was an ordained minister at Zion Temple #1. His first wife was Adline Sain. His second wife was Ollie his third wife was Lovie. She was considerably younger than grandpa. They divorced, and Ms. Lovie got a house and a piece of land from the divorce. His fourth wife was Hattie Crisp. Ms. Hattie had been married before to a preacher.

She talked about how Grandpa John West loved his cheese, bananas, and vegetables. He did not like sweets. He would travel and drag his truck around, partly everywhere he went, with his newspapers and hook cheese in it.

Aunt Lil says John West was not of the dark skin Indians. She traveled to Nashville, Tennessee and saw some of the relatives.

Sandra went on to tell me that in 1880, Dick was thirty years old; an African American man. Apparently, this must be the man that Sandra's mom spoke of when Grandpa's mother left him, and he took Grandpa and his half-sister in. Dick got Mary Curry pregnant after taking her in at age 16. They had two children together. End of interview.

In my interview with Junious, when grandpa attended to school, the teacher felt she was not spelling his name correctly. The way grandpa's last name should have been spelled. Even today it is my understanding his last name is misspelled.

Rev. John West McTizic (Grandpa) feeding the chickens (1966)

I recall my grandpa living down a back road way down past Mt. Olive cemetery. He used to eat those runny eggs. Therefore, he kept the chickens fed. Momma and Daddy would pick him up almost every Saturday and take him to town. We stopped at a store along the highway outskirts of town on the left side. This was where he shopped. And the man in the store would ask him, "How old are you, Mr. West?" "One Saturday, he would say, "Aw, ninety-three." The following Saturday, the store owner would ask again, "How old are you, Mr. West?" Grandpa would say, "Aw, ninety-two and a half." The store owner would get such a kick out of him. Grandpa had a plenty of sense.

He used to walk a lot. And he would come from a walk and sit in the chair backward with his backside to the old warm heater.

I think back to my visiting my grandpa's home. He played his old fiddler. He would then let out a sound from his mouth as he tuned up the fiddle. But I never did hear a song sung. All I ever heard was *aw, aw, aw.* I was told he really could play the fiddle very well. Sources told me that he was raised by a white man and had been married four times.

Second wife   Fourth wife

I can remember several times hearing how he had an old mare. And one day he wanted to go to town. He got in the buggy and said; "Getty' up" well, no "Getty up happened. Grandpa stepped down from the buggy and bit the old mare on the ear. He got back in the buggy and said, "Getty-up!" They proceeded to town.

I wonder if John West was three years old when he waved goodbye to his mother in 1865, as reported. This was when the civil war was over, and slaves were freed. He was born in 1870 according to his headstone. That would have made him five years old at the time the slaves were freed in 1865.

It is my understanding when Grandpa West grew up and married Grandma Ollie; Aunt Mary Jones was the eldest child. If it is true that Aunt Mary Jones was treated as an outside child, could this child have been born to Adline, Grandpa's first wife, and Grandma Ollie and Grandpa West raised her?

If the censors showed that the child was four years old at the time, I am wondering whose child it was. Or was there really an outside child and the censors were wrong? Then I thought maybe Grandpa and Grandma could have taken in this child who possibly belonged to another sibling? If so, could this sibling have died? Who were they?

We do know that Mary Curry and Grandpa West were not full sister and brother. Could someone be holding information and not want to talk about it like Aunt Lil did with her granddaughter about Aunt Mary Jones? It does not matter at this point.

Since Grandma Ollie had sisters, I guess it is possible that the four-year-old could be one of Ollie's sister's children, and she and Grandpa raised her. Better yet, is this Grandma and Grandpa's child together, and possibly was pregnant before marriage, and this was the way it showed up on the censor's report?

There are so many unanswered questions. I can understand that a sixteen-year-old can work. But how could a mother leave a three to five year old child? This is puzzling to me. Was she forced to leave him? The way my sources described grandpa and his half-sister they did not feature each other. It crossed my mind that possibly his claim to be mother Caroline wasn't his real mother. His sister Mary C was tall and dark Grandpa was rather short and with a very light complexion. Sibling's does not always look alike. We must do further research in hopes of coming up with an answer. All the memories and love for family is all that matters anyway.

After getting interviews from my elder sisters and brothers, I began to look back at each story. I know Momma and Daddy were young when they married. And they were learning how to be parents as we all have. With them having thirteen children, it must have been rather stressful trying to take care of them. I say this because we were living on land that belonged to someone else. From my brothers interview my parents did not know whether the woman had died; stop paying her taxes or sold her property. Postal mailing was the only way of communicating. After trying to reach her "to no avail", this must have caused more stress.

There they were with all of these children, and Momma always found enough flour to make biscuits for the landlady and her friend when they came to collect. As you could see, in the old house story, we were forced to move. Thank goodness that Momma's daddy had a house to take us in.

Life was hard when farming was our only source of income. Sometimes, the crops made good, and, sometimes, they did not. At one point, I thought Daddy was just a man who did not pay his rent. I have been confused about the real truth growing up. Since I was only three years old when we moved to grandpa's house, I relied on what I was told by others.

But as a teenager, I remember, in the new house, Daddy showed a lot of responsibility. He paid the taxes, fed us, clothed us, kept us safe, and we never had a shut-off notice for the lights. Therefore, I can only go on what I have seen in my time spent with my dad.

Chastising was a term used in our household when we were growing up. Many of us in the family and in the south used the term beat or whipped. It is called abuse in today's society. What do we call abuse? Is abuse in the eye of the beholder as we have often heard the phrase beauty is in the eye of the beholder?

This also applies to bulling. When you have people that bully I notice that they have no respect for others at all.

We have often heard from our parents, if you spare the rod, you spoil the child. What does that really mean? The many years of the way they were taught by their parents I am pretty sure this was embedded in their minds. Did it stem from slavery?

In many cases, it probably does. Slaves were beaten, and it was accepted to be right by the slave owners. What is abuse? It is to hurt by treating badly, injury, unjust, to use wrongly. Abuse is abuse. It does not matter whether it is physically or mentally. And it does not matter who is doing the abusing. Now, today, abuse is being discussed by all races. Do you realize that people who abuse you mentally sometimes do not recognize that they are really abusing? Why?-because they feel you are to accept it. Abuse is something a person should not be forced to accept.

Years ago the media did not cover bullying and abuse as they do today. As much as we get frustrated with the attention and bad news the media covers, we must give them credit for covering stories that bring awareness to bullying and abuse. This can shed some light on the problems we face every day. This can help not only the abused but maybe stop the abusers.

We knew our parents loved us. We also knew that they had a hard time with their own struggles. We knew they gave and demanded respect. They raised us not to be liars and be lazy but to always pray and keep God in our lives. When we were mischievous or rebellious or when we disobeyed, we got our punishment. There wasn't much of a lack of respect in those parts because it was never allowed from the time your little feet hit the floor. You were taught to respect your elders. Well let's face it; give respect and earn respect!

It seems as though our society now is eliminating the words respect and honor. Our children are getting lost in this. I am not saying all children. It starts with the grownups. Teach and set good positive examples, and maybe we can get better results. It starts at home. We as parents should not base all the bad things that happened in our lives to be passed on to our children.

This applies to teaching whether in a public place or in the home. I heard something on television in an interview about a police department. And when I heard an ex-officer say that if you report to higher-ups with a problem, you are called a snitch or you are treated as an outcast, something to that affect. Call me old fashioned, and call me confused, but isn't this what our law enforcement rings out to our young people in the communities? We should not have double standards about speaking up to solve problems. Again, I feel examples set, results accomplished.

My parents were not perfect. My husband and I are not perfect parents. And who makes that decision on who is the perfect parent? Everyone has their opinion on who is perfect at anything. Sometimes, you have to be there, be in it, step back, look at the situation, and then make your decision. And even then would it be the right decision?

I am not talking about assuming or living in a similar household or situation. Every household, every parent, every situation, and everyone's way of thinking will be different. Do not get so angry at the next person because you cannot convince them to see, think, or be like you. Sometimes, we have the tendency to take after our parents and do better, and, sometimes, we choose not to. Have you heard that life is what you make of it? Since it is your life, start believing in yourself first.

Well I had to make my mind up throughout the years. I either had to know what was real and what was not. My mom and dad told scary stories to us as a way of having fun. This was better than watching the scary movies on television. We did not have a television until a few months before momma died.

I'll never forget how frightened I was as a little girl. We did not have electric lights at the time. I was afraid to take a lite oil lamp light into the kitchen. Daddy would tell those frightening stories about dead people. Then he would dare us to take the challenge. One night, he offered me one dollar to take the oil lamp and put it on the kitchen table. I was afraid of my shadow, and some of this was from some of the elder siblings frightening me.

One night, he told the story about this dead man who lived humped over all the time before he died. At that time, they did the dressing of the dead in those old homes. He said it was dark. The undertaker put a strap around the man so that he could lie straight. He had the man there strapped in on a board, he thought. When the undertaker turned his back to do something, the strap broke. The dead man sat up, and his arms went around the undertaker's neck. It frightened the undertaker some awful.

And Momma told the story how the moon was shining one night, and she stepped outside. She stepped out in the moonlight, and she saw a man coming up the road. Therefore, she stepped back a couple of feet into the shadow near the house. It was then that she noticed the man walking by; it was our deceased Uncle Nolan.

After all those type of stories, they made us all afraid. I knew I couldn't take that lamp in the kitchen after those stories. So did Daddy.

Of course, my brave brother, Carnell said "Ah, girl gone take the lamp in the kitchen and get the money. He said to Daddy, "Give me the lamp and the money. I'll take the lamp into the kitchen."

So Daddy looked over at him. He told Carnell, "Since you are so brave, I'll give you five dollars to take a lantern to Mt. Olive Cemetery and sit it on the grave of Grandma Ollie, and leave it there. I'll pick it up in the morning."

This way, by Carnell leaving the lantern, Daddy would know he actually left it there. Just think now; if he left the lantern, he would have to walk back in the pitch dark without a light. My brother not thinking this out very clearly said, "Okay, I'll do it. Just light the lantern."

Well, Daddy got the lantern and made sure it was enough oil in it. He turned it down low so that the oil did not burn out before he got there. So, Carnell took the lantern in his hand. He got his brave side all worked up. When he stepped out on the porch, we closed the door.

Daddy stood up, and Momma started laughing. Momma must have known Daddy wasn't up to any good when she began to laugh. Daddy went out the backdoor and down to the barn; Carnell, in the meantime, was walking rather slowly, and that night, it was pitch dark. There wasn't any moonlight or stars shinning.

Walking slowly and carefully, looking and listening, Carnell had gotten even with the barn on the dirt road. Daddy made the cows go moo and the mules kick the stale doors. Daddy took off running back to the house. He barely made it and sat in the chair. He was out of breath. Momma was laughing so hard. Therefore, we laughed too. We were enjoying momma and daddy having fun.

We could hear Carnell's footsteps. He was running so fast. He did not say, "Open the door." He said loudly, "Open door, open door." We had the door open for him. He ran so fast I want to say he must have missed the steps and the porch.

You see, Daddy thought he was really going through with it. So he had to do something before his son could earn this money. Daddy did not have five dollars in the first place. Carnell was out of breath, and Daddy was too. We all had a good laugh with that one.

So much for Daddy telling us scary stories; my sister Ethel told me how Mr. Spinks had died. Daddy, being the helpful man he was and being so supportive, decided to go help dress this dead man. After he had helped and did a good deed, he headed home. Keep in mind, it was pitched dark. And the only light in the country was moonlight or the stars. Once again, the stars and moon are not shinning.

Somewhere along the way, a white horse appeared; Daddy got frightened. Before he could reach the house, he called out with a convincing voice, "Open the door, Wesley B.! Wesley B.! Open that door!" We loved hearing these stories after a hard day's work.

We did a lot of farming. It was very hard work. Many times, we prayed for rain. Daddy and Momma prayed for the rain to help the crops grow. We, as children, prayed for rain because we did not want to go to the fields and work.

We raised fruits, vegetables, cattle, pigs, mules, and fished for a living. Quilts were made out of old clothes, etc. Watermelons, eggs, and peanuts were sold. The cotton was raised and taken to the cotton gin. Cash was given to Daddy by the pound. The corn that was raised was taken to the corn mill to make corn meal for our corn bread. Some were kept for eating and feeding the livestock.

We had a stovepipe wood stove in the kitchen and a stovepipe wood heater in the living room. When the wood burned out at night in the heater, we had so many old quilts on us to keep warm. We had so many that we couldn't turn over. You didn't have to worry about moving in a cold spot because you couldn't move. And if you did not have enough cover, you did not want to move because you did want to give up your warm spot. Who wanted to freeze to death?

In the summer, we had fun. We had a tree house. We went fishing, hunting, swimming, climbed trees, rode the mules, and played jacks, baseball, basketball, paddle and wheel, marbles, etc.

We kept busy. If we weren't playing, we worked really hard. When we could, we played with our cousins, Aunt Lil's children, who lived up the hill from us. Yes, they were poor as well. Aunt Lil's daughters, Ruthie and Ruby, played with us often. Momma and Aunt Lil's children were pretty much the same age or very close in age, and we had such good fun.

When we became of age, we went to town on Saturdays to the show. And Ruthie and I even went on dates together. Such dating it was. I think we feared our parents if we tried to date too much.

With Momma gone, Daddy was somebody to fear. It was like being branded by a hot iron in your brain, like you would brand a cow. You respected the household and the name. This is the way many of the parents tried to teach their children.

It would have been nice if they taught the children a little more about being so mischievous. I can remember the time Ruthie, Ruby, and I went to the Mt. Olive Cemetery. We were young then. They would tell me, "If you say to the grave, Come up three times, the dead will rise." I don't know if someone told them that, or they made it up. I knew I could never make myself get to the third come up. I knew I was ready to get up and run if anything moved.

On a different day, at this same cemetery, Clinora decided to go over and fool around with Grandma Ollie's headstone. It was just her and me. I stayed outside of the cemetery in the road. Grandma's headstone leaned or fell over; somehow, it started sinking down in the ground onto the grave. She got excited and wanted me to help. I nervously helped her. I was thinking that Grandma will have to finish sleeping with this on her head if I heard the first noise.

I don't know how I got pulled in on so many things. Maybe, it was because I was the youngest in the family. Of my first cousins, Ruthie was one year older than me, and Ruby was one year older than her. This made me the youngest on the hill at that time.

We enjoyed all our cousins. Any fighting and fussing between the children was controlled by the adults no matter whose child it was. The grownups did not allow it.

Aunt Minnie and her family would come down from Memphis, Tennessee. We had lots of fun with them as well. Momma and Aunt Minnie were very close. Aunt Minnie would bring out a big bag of donuts. And we ate like crazy. We stayed out in the country and did not get donuts very often. Matter of fact it was only when we went to town on Saturday. There were times we did not have the money. But when we did it was very difficult in trying to make a decision on which donut to choose was even harder. And Aunt Minnie's children looked for fresh homemade food. Momma cooked fresh corn off the cob, peas, greens, chicken, corn bread and cold lemonade. Aunt Minnie's children ate until they were miserable.

Momma got a kick out of her son, Lynn. He was a big guy and played football. He ate so much that he would lie under the shade tree and did not want his shirt to touch his stomach. When she died, Lynn took it pretty hard at the funeral.

My elder siblings made their way to Detroit. One person ended up in Cleveland. Nowadays children leave home at age eighteen. It is considered being grown. Some time ago age twenty one was considered grown. During the time my elder brothers and sisters left home they were under the age of eighteen. The eldest brother was thirteen I learned when he left home seeking work.

Many of the stories you are about to read about at the old Weaver farm are of the elder brothers and sisters since I had no memories of the old place at all. Grandpa built his house. We all piled in on him until he moved out and married again to his fourth wife. I guess with six children and two adults it was time to go.

My parents had some home remedies for almost any and everything. With them not having much money and the amount of children it was difficult for them.

Allie was telling me that James had gotten stung by a wasp or a bee. He came to the dinner table. His ear was about the size of a slice of wonder of bread. She talked about how they laughed at him. I bet no doctor.

Carl cut his foot on a thick piece of glass. The blood was shooting out as though it was a fountain pen. Momma and Daddy put some coal oil and sugar on it and wrapped it up.

Clinora went to the doctor when her finger was cut. She almost lost it. It was my understanding that Daddy was in the fields. Momma was in the house. As a little boy, Freddie was cutting some wood and Clinora wanted to put a little piece of wood or twig on the block for Freddie to cut. Well, he cut all right. He cut her finger. It was cut through down to the bone. It was dangling.

They got Daddy; he and Momma took her to the doctor. The doctor sewed it back up. It is still a little crooked even today. I am glad they made the choice to take her to the doctor. I am glad Daddy didn't decide to take a steeple and a hammer and try to put the bone back together and have Momma sew the skin back on with needle and thread. They had a plenty home remedies, but that wasn't one of them.

We were defiantly poor. We had a place to live thanks to grandpa. We owned three mules, a few cows, a few pigs, three dogs, one cat, one car, a barn, a shed, a vegetable garden, a water well, a chicken house, a smoke house, and an outside toilet. We had an orchard where grandpa had planted peach, pear, and apple trees. You could find blackberries and other fruits on the property.

All in all, we had to do without a lot of things back then.

Reflecting over the past:

Electric lights (about a year before Momma died in 10/4/1965)

Telephone (not before Momma's death)

Running water (none-no pipes)

Television (a few months before Momma's death)

Used outdoor toilet- no rush-no flush

Wringer washing machine (purchased for mother's day, passed October of same year)

Smokehouse (stored meat from the pigs/hogs)

1946 black Ford

Fish

Flour (purchased 25-pound bag used for bread; sack used to make clothes—Mom would pick the prettiest pattern.)

Hunting/trapping (rabbits, coons, squirrels, opossums)

Chicken house (chickens & eggs kept)

Cows (milk & butter)

Corn (ground up for corn meal for corn bread)

> Syrup and molasses—(There were times Momma made syrup out of water and sugar.)
>
> Peanuts (planted and sold)
>
> Vegetables (vegetable garden—canned and frozen foods—Momma got a freezer shortly before her death.)
>
> Fruit (orchard—canned fruits for the winter)
>
> Coffee & sugar (purchased)
>
> Popcorn (raised our own)
>
> Walnut trees (eating and cooking)

Many of our clothes were made. Momma ordered some things from Sears and National Belles Hess catalogs. We called this credit. They called it on time.

I was told that Daddy made a pair of shoes once, but they were too hard to wear. I am willing to bet that he tried them on first. If it was any way possible, he could have worn them; he would have been making us wear hard shoes until we moved out. But, again, this might have helped us to move out a little faster.

We did not have everything we wanted. We had some of what we needed. But we made it with what we had.

The mules we had were dependable animals, except maybe Daisy. I barely can remember our mare Daisy. I can remember Dick, Ada, and Kate. They were working mules for the field. Daddy worked Ada and Dick more than he did Kate. Kate worked Daddy instead Daddy working Kate. Smart man don't you think! She was always in a hurry. No one was anxious to ride her either.

I rode Dick a couple of times but I wasn't too comfortable. Riding Kate was out of the question for me. I know people use saddles on horses. I never rode with a saddle until I came to Detroit. But of course I rode horses in Detroit.

Ada

Ada was the only one I was comfortable riding. She was easy and gentle. She was very smart. The good part was she never was in a hurry. I felt at peace when I rode her. She was something special.

However, you ride mules and horses, not a cow; unless you are in a rodeo. Girl age 10 with their white face cow. Age of the cow is unknown. Upon a visit by her sister one year she took this picture. She mailed the girl a copy with five dollars enclosed.

She stated; "I am not sure who needs the five dollars the most because you and the cow are poor as heck" only she used a little stronger word.

Dick

Now, Dick and Daddy had a relationship. If Daddy was talking to someone while they were in the fields, Dick would not move. Daddy can say, "Get up mule." Dick would not move because Daddy was still talking. Now, Daddy can stop talking and say nothing; old Dick will go.

And at the end of the day, Daddy would take Dick to the barn. Once he got in the stable, he would take his head and push the door open. He wanted to be fed. He kept doing it until Daddy gave him some corn. I think they could have had a man-and-the-mule show together. They knew each other well.

The dogs were dependable as well; so was my black cat named Jack. My cat would wake me up in the morning before school. He jumped up on the foot of my bed and crawled his way up to my face and woke me up at six o'clock.

Sam, Rock, and Hunter are the dogs I can recall. We did not own all the dogs at the same time. I later had a dog. His name was Timmy, a beagle. I only had him for a short time. But I guess he figured it wasn't any need for both of us being poor.

So he left home. I guess somebody else was feeding him. Sam was a good hunting dog. Arthur had a dog named Spot. It is my understanding, every time Momma whipped my brother Arthur, the dog would bite at her stockings. I bet old spot didn't try that with Daddy. If he had, every dog, cat, and mule on the hills would be gone. This included him.

Later came along old Rock and old Hunter. Rock was a pretty brown-and-black dog with more hair than Hunter. I didn't think Rock was as aggressive as Hunter either, but he was a good hunting dog.

Strange dogs are a dog sometimes to be afraid of but a mad dog is something to stop you in your tracks. It is my understanding that Momma was afraid of mad dogs, the mentally ill when they wandered out of the facility, and tornadoes. Now, if you look at the three mentioned, who would not be afraid? Carl was telling me about how, one time, at the old house, a bad tornado came through. Momma took all the children and put them in a corner and covered them with her body and stayed there with them until the tornado passed.

I recall Mr. Bossy and his wife would always go to someone's house every time it was a tornado that was coming. They have been to our house as well. When the tornado is over, they would drive back home. It was because his wife had been blown away in a storm once. I can understand why the visits. But, what the wife did not realize, Momma was just as afraid as she was of a tornado.

Columbus was telling me once about this man that wandered away from the Western State Mental Institution in Bolivar. The institution was built in 1889 and set outside of Bolivar. In the 1960s, it housed over two thousand patients. It was the last state mental hospital to be built in Tennessee. And when you mention where you were from, people would say, "Oh yea, that crazy house down there." They thought we were all crazy who lived in Bolivar because of the institution.

Daddy was walking through the woods. He wandered upon a man. This incident was at the old place. This man was staying in the woods. He was standing there eating the green leaves off a bush. Allie said she remembered seeing the man. He had a beard. She recalled peeping in through the branches at him.

Daddy would take the man food. Finally, he got the authorities to come get him. I guess with Daddy feeding him, this kept the man from coming to the house. I can imagine if, he had followed Daddy to the house, Momma would have been sending food to Daddy and the man in the woods.

Another time, there was a woman that came to our house. This was also at the old place. This woman had leaves in her clothes and in her hair. The woman walked up to the porch. Momma put her children behind her and told Freddie and Clinora to go get Daddy. Clinora said she could barely keep up with Freddie. Everybody was afraid.

Daddy dropped what he was doing and came to the house. This was the sister of a man daddy knew. Daddy hitched the mules to the wagon and went to notify the man of his sister. They took her back to the Western State Hospital. It seemed as though it was a few that wandered off from the hospital. The security for the hospital is safer now than years ago. The hospital is still in business.

MEMORIES OF OUR PARENTS

Wesley B.   Arthur

WHEN YOU LOSE A love one you cannot imagine the void until they are gone. Life goes on for you but voids are sometimes never filled. Love ones will be gone but not forgotten. It is these types of stories and memories that will stay with you forever. What a blessing to have. Everyone cannot share such memories. No one should miss out on love. We should capture each moment of life. The love you shared and precious moments certainly stays with a person their lifetime. This is why it is so important how we live our lives and most of all what kind of memories we are leaving behind for others. You never know whose life you can touch before you leave this world.

James

Wesley B. believed in education for her children. She took a stand so that they could have some education. In my interview with my brother James, he says, momma was pretty much a pioneer for education.

His interview was very enlightening. He recalls Momma having gone to the courthouse in town in Bolivar letting the authorities know that the other school, Pine Grove, was too far for her children to walk to school. It was about six miles from where we lived. It was a one-room house where Momma and Daddy had gotten married in. Momma suggested this house for her children and other children to go to school in the area. She helped many people in that community.

He says he wanted to quit school, and Momma said, "No!" Her words were "You might work in a warehouse someday." And lo and behold he ended up working in one after moving to Michigan.

He remembers one occasion when Daddy whipped him for something Daddy thought he had done. But, indeed, it was his elder brother. It was some type of sexual remark. Before the whipping started, James said he folded his arms like an Indian chief and told himself I will not cry. While Daddy was whipping him, he, all of a sudden, stopped. Daddy told Momma that he was innocent, and he would never whip him again.

He recalled, one time in the kitchen, the window was open. He was begging Momma for something that our parents could not afford. Daddy was outside of the window listening.

Momma had a stick of stove wood in her hand. James said that Momma could see that he was not going to stop begging, so she took the piece of wood and swung it at him and he ducked. The wood missed him and hit Daddy.

I asked; "James what did you do?" His response was "I left the kitchen and went into the woods." This was one time, I can say, he did not whip me. He kept his word. End of interview

It appears that the wood did all the whipping and saved James. Momma worked hard in the best way she knew how to make ends meet for the sake of her family. She was a praying woman who believed in God and that God would provide. Momma instilled this in her children.

West

In my interview with West he remembered momma as saying' "God will not put no more on you than you can bear." She was a good cook and a hard worker.

He remembers daddy as saying' when he would see someone do something wrong my dad would say' that scrounger should know better. He recalls the times daddy brought home old Dick our mule. At first daddy was a little Leary of the mule. West says he jumped up on the mule and rode him around a few times putting his foot out to make a stirrup for his younger brother James to climb on. Daddy was impressed. End of interview

Allie

After interviewing my elder sister, Allie, she was telling me how one time she had visited home in the month of August. The weather was so very hot during that time. She says she told Momma that it was entirely too hot, and she was going back to Michigan and come back to visit at Christmas time.

Momma was sitting in a chair shelling some peas. Allie says she was lying on the ground on a pallet. Momma told her without looking up, "I won't be here." Allie said to Momma, "Aw, Momma, stop talking like that." Momma continued talking and said, "I want your daddy to remarry. I want you to take Mable and Cody and raise them together." "Why are you choosing me to raise them?" Her response was "I don't want them separated."

She remembers Momma being full of love. She knew Momma had an arm out of this world. She has seen the time when Momma would ease out the backdoor when she saw a rabbit and carefully take a piece of wood and throw at the rabbit and kill it. That would be our dinner.

She thought back to when Momma had dreamed the same dream three nights in a row. In the dream, there were angels. They lifted her up and pointed to a grave at the Mt. Olive

Cemetery. Not long after the dream, her mother, Grandma Ollie died.

She remembers daddy as being a hard working father. Even today she cannot figure out how he took care of his large family with one plow, one mule, and one ax.

She spoke of how she and our sister Idell had visited Daddy one day. They rode to the cemetery to visit Momma's grave. Daddy looked back at the grave and said, "It won't be long now, Wesley B.! It won't be long!" End of interview

Eunice

My interview with Eunice came as a surprise to me. She remembers momma as loving and compassionate. Eunice recalls the time when she was skinny and did not eat properly. Momma made different foods trying to get her to eat. One afternoon when she and her other siblings were coming home from school, Eunice was the last one to come up the road. She says momma would stand on the porch until she could see her coming. Once she saw her she would go back in the house.

After Eunice arrived home she laid down. Momma was so worried about her because the polio was going around. Our mom thought she had the polio.

She remembers daddy as the kind of father that worked hard to provide for his family. He was good about helping others. Jokes were always on daddy's list every chance he got. End of interview

Ethel

In interviewing my sister Ethel, she was telling me how she had pulled her tooth and was rinsing her mouth with Momma's one and only glass. She dropped the glass and broke it. Momma had told her to put the glass up because she had rinsed her mouth enough. Ethel says she doesn't remember Momma playing baseball, but she had a dead aim with a boot and caught her in the bend of her knees.

She recalls daddy as being a hard working father. Ethel says she and Momma wrote each other often. This letter was written in August, 1956 when her husband asked for her hand in marriage (end of interview).

2

you and Ethel mae was in
loue. you know the
Bible Say who so euer &
Join togeather let not
Man put assunder.
So their for we could not
obgect for if you to are in
loue its god will
S hope Both of you have
Made it up in you Mind
to settle Down and Devote
your selues to each other
you know the Bible Say
let euery Man have his
own wife and euery Woman
her own husband &
hope that you have the loue
for her that god loues
when he said Man loue

Your wife like god love the church that he gave his life for it and again I say I wont her to be Opediance to you as god say wemons obey your husband. for this is right. hoping you all a great Suscess Hope to meet you in the near future from Mr & Mrs Orthur Weaver

Clinora

My sister Clinora remembers Momma saying the Lord will make a way out of no way, and the lord will provide. Also how Momma taught her how to sew and cook. She recalls Momma as hard working and sold chickens for money.

She also remembers momma as being an advocate for education. If it wasn't for her speaking out about the distance for the children to travel six miles in the community she might not have started the second grade at Bolivar Industrial Elementary School.

She remembers Daddy plowing the fields and cutting wood. What stood out for her was Daddy's whistling. His favorite songs were "Farther Along" and "Sweet Home." When he whistled momma would say hush now so I can hear your daddy. End of interview

Carl

My Brother Carl's interview really touched my heart. He said Momma and Daddy did not have hidden secrets. He recalled Momma letting him have a vegetable garden of his own. He knew that Momma was very proud of all her children. And when he did get a whipping from her for something he knew he shouldn't have done, Daddy was the best cheerleader in town. Daddy would say pour it to him!

When Carl got drafted into the army at age eighteen, this is when he learned that Momma had died. He had just finished with his basic training. As far he knew, she was fine and had not been ill. When he got the news, he was in shock.

He says, being a young green country boy who only had been to school and to town, it was hard adjusting to the army life and hearing of your mother's death all happening at once. He felt that it was too much for one person to take on at such a young age. Carl said everything was happening so fast because when he arrived back at the base, the people in charge told him that he did not have to be shipped out if he did not want to because his mom had died. He told them I'll go ahead because this is what she would have wanted me to do.

He is grateful that he made that decision. Had he not gone on and took the shipment to Germany, the next shipment was going to be Vietnam. He remembered Daddy as a man of perfection. If you mess up, he would tear you up.

Carl talked about how good of a shot Daddy was. He says Daddy took the 22 rifle with fourteen bullets and came back with thirteen squirrels. What a team he and Momma made. She had an arm like a baseball pitcher. He was also good at shooting. Both parents loved us all. End of interview

Cody

You will see throughout my stories that Cody and I were very close in growing up together. He recalls how he begged Daddy to let him plow the rows in the fields. Daddy explained to him, "Now, you go up this side of the row and back down the other the row."

After getting it wrong three or four times, Daddy told him, "Give me the plow. I tell you, your memory ain't long as your nose, and these rows are crooked, worse than a dog's hind legs."

He remembered Momma having all those pretty flowers. He could picture her sitting under the shade tree. She used to eat soak stone (white hard dirt-something like starch). How Momma would work in the fields with us and leave early to prepare dinner or lunch. And when she got it ready, she would yell, "Yeeehoooo," for us to come to the house to eat. It did not matter how far away we were, we could hear her. Both of them could look at the sun and tell the time. End of interview

Mable

My memories of Momma were her having an unbelievable kindness about her and the patience of Job as in the bible. She loved her children and her grandchildren dearly. If she could have, she would have raised as many of her grandchildren as she could, along with Cody and little Freddie

Momma believed in her children getting their education. And her famous biscuits and cooking go without saying. She was a woman who held her peace, and she was a praying woman. She would say, "Sometimes, you have to keep a distance for peace's sake."

I can remember how she worked so hard in the fields and in the vegetable garden. You know, it is a funny thing. Around the age of ten, I was sitting on the porch in the swing with her after a long hot day in the garden. She was wringing wet with sweat under her arms. It was stains of sweat down almost to her waist.

Being mischievous, I eased over trying to sneak and smell Momma without her knowing it. Without looking over at me, she said, "You won't smell your Momma. I sweat, but I don't smell." By her being full of sweat, I thought she would smell. And she didn't then, and as I think about it, I never have smelled her.

She ordered candy from the candy man to sell. We would eat a lot of it up. We were like little blood hounds. As long as we knew the candy was not all gone, we were trying to figure out where it was hidden. Daddy really could have used us to track down rabbits because we were as good as the dogs when it came time to track down food.

One time I found the box of candy. It was inside of an old stove. There were about eight candy bars left inside the box. I couldn't bring myself to take one because I figured momma had counted them.

She would hide from the candy man because she could not pay him on time when he came back. But the candy man would give her the candy every time she was available. The candy from the candy man was sold at the church.

One night we had a Revival at Zion Temple church number one. The healing minister came. The minister had one woman jump up some steps, flat foot. And he was healing a long line of folk. I was just looking on.

When I looked at the line near the end, I spotted Momma in the line. I got so nervous. I bet I went to the bathroom five or six times before the minister got to Momma. I looked to my left. There, Daddy was at the edge of his seat and looking on so anxiously.

After Momma had gotten a few feet away from the minister, I jumped up and went to the bathroom again. Whenever I would go, it would only be about a teaspoon full and, sometimes, nothing. I don't know why my nerves were so bad.

The last time I went out, this woman stopped me as I was leaving out. She told me I couldn't be walking that much during the service. When I sat back down, Momma was the next one up. He spoke something to Momma. She spoke something back to him. I suppose she was telling him what was wrong or the problems she was having.

All of a sudden, this minister hit Momma in the side and snatched at her shoulder. He did everything so fast. When he hit her in her side, it was as if he was angry. When he snatched at her shoulder, it was as if he saw a bug up there.

Momma ran through the front of the church, up in the pulpit, and grabbed her brother, Tommie. At this point, I don't know what Daddy was doing. I was so busy witnessing everything.

She finally, came back to her seat. I later found out that she had been having some pain in her side. She had a big knot on her shoulder. Somewhere down the line, the knot left. I never heard about the pain in her side. I do remember Momma making a statement that it is not in the healer as much as it is in the believer.

There were a few school mornings, while Momma was in the kitchen, Daddy would brush, comb, and braid my hair. As a little girl, in the mornings, I would get sick to my stomach. Daddy poured a little coffee in a saucer from his coffee cup and gave it to me before school. He told Momma that it would probably settle my stomach. It did, and I went to school. I'm sure this helped Momma out.

I can remember my daddy being one of the hardest working men I knew. He was very firm. But, he was full of fun. He showed love that you had to come to know. He loved to tell and hear jokes.

I was told that he only had a third grade of education. But he was good at math. He could look at the sun and tell the time and measure and build with his bare hands. When it came to fractions he was good at it. A few nights I had trouble with my math in fractions. He helped me. Thanks to him I finally got it.

When he made Momma real angry, he would apologize by going to town (ten miles) just to get her orange slice candy or chocolate drop candy or orange circus peanut candy. He knew these were her favorite. He would come home with a little brown bag with candy in it and give to her.

Daddy fussed quite a bit. But Momma would hang in there. She knew how to handle Daddy. She would wait until he was done. There have been times he would have been wrong. She would wait until he finally would admit it. That was not easy for him to do. I tell you, pride is something. You can hurt yourself and the next person too if you let pride stand in the way.

Let me give you an example. One time, the gate to the barn was left open. Either the cows or the mules had gotten out. Daddy fussed and fussed. He walked back and forth. Momma kept doing what she was doing and said, "Well, now, Arthur." He would continue.

Then, finally, silence from Momma. After a while, Daddy would cool off. He waited a few minutes and realized that it wasn't someone else that left the gate open. He finally broke down and said to Momma, "Wesley B., I believe I left that gate open." Again, he was not the apologizing type. But he would buy that candy.

One thing about those two, you could not play one against the other. When it came to their children, they were together on it. If you ask Momma, "Can I go to town?" She would say, "Did you ask your daddy?" You go ask Daddy, and he would say, "Well, what did your Momma say?"

You *might* eventually get to town. But if you lied, you did not go to town. And, by the time you go to town the next time, you probably would have forgotten where the town was and forgotten what the town looked like. That would be how long it would be before you go again.

We had an old bridge near the highway. It was always in need to be repaired. It was pretty shaky. There was water underneath it. When it rained pretty hard, the water would rise.

Most of the time, Momma would let me sit upfront with her and Daddy. Of course, I would sit by the window. This put Momma in the middle of me and Daddy. And when the car would go over the top of the bridge, the planks would make a noise.

Whenever we'd go to town or out for a visit, we had to come over this one and only bridge. There was no other way out. Momma was afraid of this bridge. Every time Daddy crossed over the bridge, Momma would draw up and reach over and squeeze Daddy's thigh. And Daddy laughed. Now that I am older, I think that Daddy did not want to fix that bridge too quickly. He probably would have missed those several thigh squeezes. End of my memories.

When my mom married my dad his belief was "your word is your bond." This was apparently what was taught by his parents. He was a very hard working man who was very firm, caring, and loving in his own way.

His raising was pretty much the same way. He wholeheartedly, as well as Wesley B., believed that when you stepped outside of their door, you represented the family. You were taught not to bring shame on the family. As they would put it, "you will not tarnish this name."

Well, in Ecclesiastes 7:1 it says, "A good name is better than precious ointment: and the day of death than the day of one's birth." Would it be fair to say, it's better to die with a good name than to live with a bad one?

I know you might say, "Times have changed. It's a new day. Things are different now. That's old-folk stuff. We don't do that now, Momma, Daddy, Grandma, or Grandpa." How many times have we heard those phrases? Well, we do know attitudes change, fashions change, your appearance changes, hair styles change, and it's a different era now. But one thing about it is that God has never changed. He is the same God who pulled our parents and great-grandparents through life.

We, as children growing up, at some point in time, have thought that our parents were too hard on us. They did not understand you or what you were going through. Do not think for one minute that our grand and great grandparents did not have these same feelings. Because of their parent's guidance, they too brought some of that learning experience into the raising of their children.

The further you go back in the generation and time, the more you will find that they had it a little harder than the next generation. We have done so, and you will as well. You can pick all the bits and pieces out you want; some will still be there. As Daddy would say, "Mark my word!"

We must admit to ourselves, that the groundwork was laid for us all, beginning even before slavery time. But our parents, grandparents and great grandparents, set the groundwork for us all. They wanted the schooling. They wanted to be able to vote. They fought hard for all of us so we could have that same opportunity.

Now, that all these things are laid out for us, young people should take the freedom that has been offered to them and act on it in a positive way and set some good things in place for the next generation.

Let's face it; everything our parents and grandparents have taught us, we are going to do differently. Some of those things will be good and some will not. Our young generations can read and learn from our history and set examples for their children. And perhaps someday your children will do the same thing. Time will bring about a change, and you have to make a change during that time, but, hopefully, it's for the best.

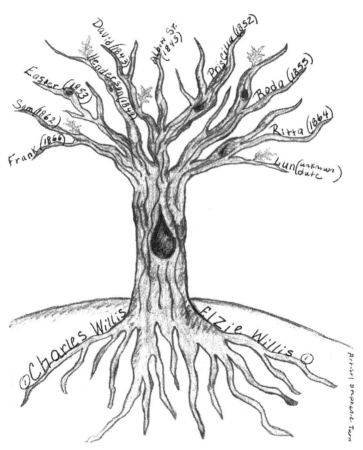

Tree Illustrated by Stephanie Turner

A poem for Charles

Slavery Time

You were born a slave and wanted to be free;

At that time in the 1800s, it wasn't meant to be.

Held back and used as a slave,

Died and buried in your grave.

The hard times, you suffered, for your family,

Denied freedom, simply because Master did not want you free.

Family members and friends went through the same thing,

Must have been hard, to reframe.

Because of your sufferings, abuse and more,

You helped your children with suffering and opened a door.

So, thank you, Grandma and Grandpa
for all that you had to endure,

Laying the ground work for this family for sure.

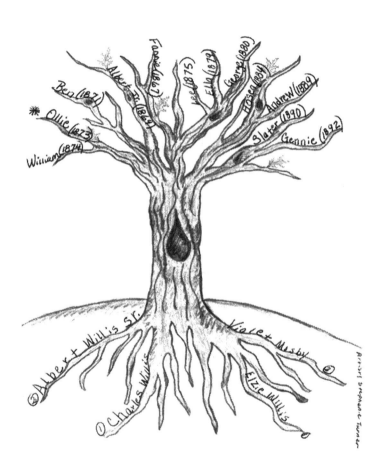

A poem for Albert

Search for Freedom

You were born as a slave in 1845,

No place to run and no place to hide.

Came over on a boat, with your father and your mother,

Lived in Hornsby, Tennessee, and did not move any further.

Stayed in the country, possibly in the sticks,

Sold on an auction block at the tender age of six.

You met Grandma at an early age,

Did not look back, just turned the next page.

She was twelve, and you were fourteen;

Married each other because of the love in between.

Slavery must not have been any easier, for either of you;

But, I am grateful; you made it through.

So, thank you, Grandma and Grandpa, for what you've done,

Setting things in place; so this generation does not have to run.

Pictured are Mr. and Mrs. Willis Sr.
(This is according to my cousin Josie Brown.)

Olevia, daughter of Albert   Octava, daughter of Albert
and Violet Willis   and Violet Willis

Born October 20, 1875 Born March 18, 1888
Died March 21, 1896 Died May 7, 1898
Come to rest Home at peace
Located at the Hornsby Cemetery

Father-in-law of Wesley B. (Marion in casket & wife, Anna, in black)
Marion was killed by a bull in 1922.
The boy in white cap is believed to my dad.

In 1922, there was a write-up in the newspaper in Hardeman County stating that Marion Weaver was killed by a bull. It spoke of how respectable of a colored man he was. I was told how he would sell eggs and sometimes give the eggs on credit to some people. One day he entered the barnyard, the bull decided to turn on him. He pulled out his insides. He did not make it. Clinora searched the censors. He was listed at age 17 as a mulatto servant. Mulatto is an offensive term of someone who has both; black and white parent or ancestors.

The headstone of Wesley B.'s mother-in-law Nov. 12, 1865-Aug. 1, 1931

It is my understanding that Grandma Anna did not take much crap. She did not fool around. People talked about how smooth and pretty her skin was.

Rev. John Wesley McTizic buried in Mount Olive Cemetery, Bolivar, Tennessee (1870-1969)

Ollie Willis McTizic buried in Mount Olive Cemetery Bolivar, Tennessee (1874-1948)

Misprint Wesley B. Dec 18, 1911-Oct 4, 1965

DREAMS

WHEN I WAS ABOUT fifteen years old, I was asleep in my bed in the back bedroom. I saw Momma so plainly. She was floating in the air at the foot of my bed. She waved her arm one time across my bed as if she was blessing me.

I told Daddy about it the next day. He was most interested in the dream. He wanted to know, if Momma said anything. I told him, "No, she didn't, Daddy." But, after that, I had a kind of peace come over me. It is amazing how dreams can show you things. Sometimes, it seems as though things are shown to you before it really happens.

After, I was all grown up; I recall having a dream about Idell one Saturday night, after she had passed. It was so real. I called Allie up that Sunday and told her about my dream. It was so plain. Idell called me on the telephone (in my dream) and she was lying down. She told me, I have to come back. I forgot somebody. She hung up the telephone. Not long, a few weeks after that, our first cousin, Eugene, closer to Idell's age, died.

This is another dream I had. I called Allie and Clinora and told them about this dream. In my dream, Allie and I were walking from the yard to the porch of our new house. There was a man walking with us into the house. I did not recognize the man. The man never spoke a word, nor did we.

As I stepped onto the porch, I looked over my left shoulder. This woman was standing off at a distance. I was trying to figure out who she was.

Allie, the man, and I went on into the house. This man led the way; Beck followed, and I entered the house last. We looked around in the front room. There were blood splatters in the room. Nobody said a word. We just looked around and came back outside.

The man did not come out with us. He kind of disappeared. As Allie and I returned back on the porch, I looked to my right. There, this woman was again. I hunched Allie and nodded in that direction. I kept looking at her.

Finally, the woman started motioning, waving her hand for me to come to her. I started walking in her direction. The closer I got, the more she start backing up. She wouldn't let me get close to her. But the closer I got, the better I could see her.

I realized then that it was our deceased mother. Just as I approached her, right where she was standing, all of a sudden, she disappeared.

I had come to the edge of a cliff. I looked down to my right. There, Momma was looking up at me. She was motioning both of her arms as if to say, "Welcome!" She would welcome me and rub her chest. She would welcome me again and rub her chest. She did that a couple of times. As she repeated it, she was shaking her head from side to side, as if she was hurting.

When I looked next to her, she was pointing to five graves. Two of those graves were covered graves, as if two people were already buried. The other three graves were open, already-dug graves.

I took it that the covered graves were Daddy and Idell since they were already dead. But the three open graves were going to be someone very close and dear to her heart. And it was going to be painful (end of dream).

Sure enough, Columbus died. Carnell died, and Freddie died later. I took it to be that the open graves were her three sons. The blood splatter we saw in the room must have been that of Carnell because he used to have some bleeding; at least, this is what I witnessed in the restroom at the hospital upon my visits with him. These three deaths in this dream occurred sometime before the three brothers had even gotten sick to my knowledge.

After the death of Carnell, I saw him in a room in this house. It appeared to be Freddie's house. It was made just like his house where he lived off a seven-mile road here in Detroit. He was shouting. And he was going around and around in a circle.

I heard a car pull up. When I looked out the side door, the car was backing up in the driveway. As the car backed up, I heard the car door close. It was a black car.

A man got out. He walked to the back of the car. I was trying so hard to see who it was. But I couldn't make out who he was. The man raised the backdoor to the car. He pulled out a casket. He draped the casket over his left shoulder. He came through the side door with the casket.

I thought he was coming to get Carnell since he was already dead and was shouting in this house. When the man put the casket down, I noticed who it was. By this time, Carnell disappeared. When I finally looked at the man, I discovered that it was Freddie. He put the casket down. He never spoke a word, nor did I (end of dream).

Freddie died later. I wondered if this was some way that he was letting me know that he would be leaving us.

When my brother-in-law, Pete, was in the hospital, I went to see him. I recall Cody kneeling down in front of him. I left the hospital that day with my heart heavy. Idell had died in this very hospital. My memories went back to her testimony when I arrived to see her when she was coming out of recovery.

I found out she was back in the hospital. I went straight from work. When I arrived to see her, she motioned for me to come in. She had white foam around the corner of both sides of her mouth. She was talking so fast, as if she couldn't tell me fast enough what she had just experienced. She asked me to contact Clinora and have her write what she had experienced.

I knew, for years, that Cody and Pete were very close. I laid down a little early this particular night. I had to go to work the next day. I dreamed that I entered a house down the street from Unity Baptist Church on Tireman Street. This house was on the side street down from the church. It was about midway of the block. I've never seen or been to this house before.

Outside, the weather was nice. It was kind of quiet. I entered this house. As I walked in, everything was completely white. In the middle of the floor was Pete sitting in a straight chair. There was no other furniture or anything on the walls. The walls were white. He had on all white. There were two who I thought to be nurses with all white on as well.

No one spoke a word. Pete was sitting there with his head down. I stood there and looked at him. He never raised his head. He never spoke a word either. Nor did I speak. I turned my head to the right of me when Pete finally raised his. When I turned to look to see what or who Pete was looking at, it was Daddy. Mind you, Daddy was already dead.

Daddy walked over to Pete and looked at him. Daddy did not say a word. But Pete nodded his head as if to say yes.

I turned and walked through the front door out onto the porch. The wind was blowing the leaves slightly. It was a calm gentle breeze. There was a Hearse in the driveway (end of dream).

Ethel called me early the next morning. I had just told my husband and daughter about the dream when the telephone rang. I believe I said to her, "Pete's gone." She asked if anyone had called me. I told her, "No, I had just dreamed it the night before."

One time, Arthur told me he had a dream about himself and Freddie. He said, in this dream, they were on this back road behind our new house. This is the road where the Bolden family lived. He claimed he and Freddie were riding on this hospital gurney. They were together rolling down this hill on this road.

The gurney picked up speed. Arthur said he jumped off on the side of the road. But Freddie stayed on. He asked me, "What do you think this could mean?" I told him maybe this means somebody might be in trouble.

Arthur replied with great concern and said, "But Freddie stayed on. It could be me." I told him, "It could but-" He cut me off. Immediately, Arthur replied, "Yea, that's what I was thinking. And we laughed it off." Freddie left him all right. He died first.

He was with him for a while on the ride, as he was in life. He was going to be leaving him behind. (end of conversation).

Allie was telling me how Arthur called her up on the telephone out of the clear one day. It was just out of the blue and about a month before he died. In the conversation, he told how he had purchased a recliner chair. Then he told her, "Well, Allie, I have outlived two wives and two children." She figured that Arthur felt his death was coming soon.

It is a funny thing about life and death. I know you have heard that statement; death is a part of living. There are two things for certain. You will live and you will die. Sometimes, you have warnings and sometimes not, or we just do not pay attention to the warnings.

I had an older lady tell me that some dreams are visions. It is a way that God is getting you prepared before it happens. I guess we should pay more attention to our dreams or visions as we should pay attention to the way our body feels. There just might be a message or warning there for you.

DETERMINATION

MY FAMILY AS MANY others in the south did what they could for survival. You have to understand country living and a determination for survival. My family had that determination simply because they had to search for food in order to have a meal.

Ethel and Eunice decided to go opossum hunting one night. They put on some boots, and off they went. Eunice was in the front. One of the brothers was in the back. And Ethel told me she was afraid, so she got in the middle.

One of the dogs chased the opossum up the tree. They all got together and shook the tree until it fell to the ground. The dog got him, and they put him in a sack. After carrying him to the house, the opossum was left in the sack until the next day. This is when they killed, cleaned, and cooked him determined to have a meal! This was one animal and the coon I could not bring myself to eat.

When I was just a little girl, Momma went out to the barn to milk the cow. It is my understanding from Carl that Momma was sitting on the stool while milking. I was standing near. I reached out to rub or touch the cow.

The cow kicked Momma, and the cow's foot got caught in her dress somehow. Off the stool, Momma fell to the ground. She got back up and continued to milk the cow. Milk had to reach the table for drinking, making butter, butter milk, and cooking. She did not stop, just determined!

Sand skitters are faster than a lizard. A lizard is usually brown and rough skinned like an alligator. A sand skitter is striped and looks something like a snake. One day, our cousin, Charles, Carl, and another cousin believed to have been Luther, were standing around next to an old log talking. A sand skitter ran up Charles's pant leg. I guess the sand skitter thought his leg was a tree. Carl says he danced worse than James Brown. But he was determined to get him out after he took his pants off!

At the old place, Carnell and Carl were trying to kill this squirrel that had run up a tree. They were in the woods just shooting up all the bullets trying to kill this one squirrel. The dog had run him up the tree. They were continuing to bark.

So Daddy decided to come down where they were. He asked why they were using up all the bullets. Daddy got the rifle and told Carl, "Just be still; don't shake." Daddy put the 22 rifle on Carl's shoulder. He aimed and shot. The squirrel didn't fall. Daddy said, "I thought sure I got him." In the next second or two, the squirrel fell to the ground. He did it with one shot—concentration and determination!

REMINISCING

A T THE OLD PLACE, Ethel and James had gone down to the spring to get some spring water. The dog started chasing a coon. The coon ran in a little cave (covey hole). The dog ran in right behind the coon. They fought and got all muddy.

James, without looking, stuck the gun inside the cave and shot. Ethel didn't know if the coon was shot or the dog. After holding their breaths, finally, the dog came out. They pulled out the coon. I guess they got water and meat that day. He could have killed the dog—A lot crazy!

On the new place, we had dams built. They were nice-sized dams. But the water was muddy and not very deep. Ethel says that James decided to go swimming. Please put in mind that James is rather tall.

He got to the edge and dived, head first. His head got stuck in the mud. His feet were up in the air. Somebody pulled him out—a little bit foolish!

Ethel claims that West went to Grandma Ollie's house with a cousin. They spent the night. He had to be back home by Sunday night so he could help Daddy in the fields the next day. Somebody had told Momma about a mad dog in the area. So when West came in that night, Momma asked, "Did you see a mad dog when you were coming this way?" West was already inside the house; it was then when he started sweating—a little bit foolish after the fact!

One Sunday afternoon, my classmate Beulah came to spend the Sunday afternoon with me. We were in the eleventh grade at the time. And I really should have known better. Daddy had gone for the evening. I rode our mule old Dick. And Beulah was to ride our mule old Ada. Ada was the gentlest mule of them all so I had her to ride Ada. When I looked back, she was running beside the mule with her arm over Ada's back as if they were best of friends.

Please do not try this! This is another case of "a hard head makes a soft behind." After putting up the mules, I decided to ride a cow. My classmate Beulah stood outside the barnyard fence with my brand new white under slip on top of her clothes. We were being silly, until . . . I decided to ride our cow.

Who knew! I was okay sitting on the cow until I adjusted myself. I can tell you, I do not remember when that cow threw me. All I remember was the ground and rolling under the barbwire fence and getting out of there.

I told Daddy about it. And he had the biggest fit and told me, "You stay out of that barn." The next day at school, both my hands were swollen pretty badly inside. I could barely write. I could have been killed—a lot foolish and a lot crazy!

Memories of
Aunts and Uncles

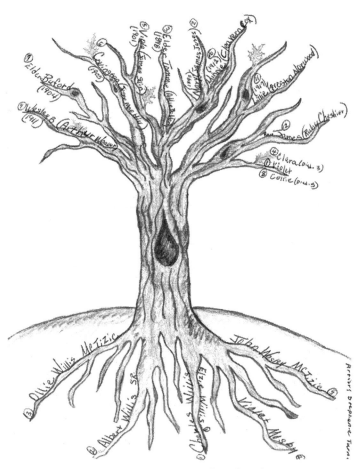

Clara, Violet, and Collie were found in the censor
report by my cousins, Sandra and Joetta.

MY MOTHER'S FOUR SISTERS and four brothers were relatives that played a great part in my life throughout the years except Aunt Mary and Uncle Covington. I did not know much about them except what I learned from other relatives. My aunts and uncles kept me in line by watching over me when my parents were not present.

During those precious days it seemed as though every teacher, neighbor, adult church member, and preacher was a parent to you. There were times our little plans did not work. There was always an adult watching. We knew that if they told our parents our story did not have a chance. And most likely the adult version was more believable anyway.

Aunt Mary, being the eldest girl, was living in Chicago way before I was born. She was a beautician. It is my understanding she never had children.

Her husband brought her back home to be buried at our Hardeman County Cemetery. My elder sister was telling me that she remembers the funeral. And that it was so very sad. The sisters took it rather hard.

Uncle Tommie was Momma's eldest brother. He became a minister and pastored a church in Bolivar, Zion Temple #1. Momma was a member of his church.

I remember going there as a little girl. His children talked about how he went back to school at a late age in Nashville. There he was being educated on opening up an adult home for the elderly. It was there that he met and saw his father's brothers.

His children spoke of how he would pass out a bag of candy, apples, and oranges during Christmas time for the children. It made not only the children happy, but their dad and mom as well. The thought that he was helping make someone else's holiday was enough for him. They spoke of how they would sit down to eat, and each one said their grace at the table.

In my interview with his son Junious, he was telling me how Uncle Tommie taught him how to set traps and catch wild animals. He said, one day, his dad purchased some sweet potato slips. And before they could plant them, the cows ate them.

He said his daddy cried. That was the first and only time that he had seen him cry. The slips cost only thirty cents, but he did not have the money to buy anymore. In those days, thirty cents was a lot of money.

Aunt Viola was described by her daughter as a virtuous woman. They talked about her taking after her mother as being a midwife. She delivered some of Momma's children. She spoke of her being a good cook and how she made the prettiest quilts.

One of her sons remember giving his mom a money tree one year and how he gave her a statue of a cat with reading glasses on it. His mom got such a kick out of that cat.

One of her daughters talked about Aunt Viola wearing false teeth. She wore them as well. So when they sat down to eat, the best eating was done without the teeth.

Her grandson Howard talked about how good she and his grandpa were to him when he was growing up. He lived on the farm with them until he finished high school.

I recall Aunt Viola and Uncle James coming to visit our house, especially every Christmas. We would go to their house as well. The special times I can remember is when they would sometime come help us in the fields, and, other times, we all would get together and have a feast.

Aunt Viola raised baby chickens in a box. She kept them in the box until they were ready to fly out. She would say to me, "Come see my baby chicks." I remember, after I had gotten grown, she made me two homemade quilts. I still have them today.

She was a very loving woman. She believed in serving God and her church. She would pray over me when I was in church. I thank her for those prayers.

Uncle Buford was also a minister following his dad's footsteps. He pastored a church, Church of God in Christ, in Hardeman County, Tennessee. He had two sisters, Lillie and Viola, who were members of his church.

One of his sons said he left home at age twelve. But he recalls his dad being a good dad. He helped him with the farming before leaving home and that his dad was a bishop for a long time.

His daughter said that she remembers how her dad would walk them to school. He was very interested in them getting their education. He made sure that they were at school on the day that the doctor's came to give shots. She talked about how he held bible studies at home on Wednesday nights.

I went to school with his youngest daughter but did not know she was a relative. I can recall one of his older daughters coming to live with us for a while. She taught me how to take a hot iron and run it over a piece of pine limb to get all the excess build up off of it.

I remember Uncle Buford as being a preacher. I remember being told that he lost his first wife while she was giving birth. He later remarried.

Uncle Covington was a brother to Momma who lived in Chicago. He was married and had one son. I never had the chance to be around this uncle to know anything much about him.

His son said so many people misunderstood him. He recalls how his dad would come to his games and cheer him on saying, "That's my son," and how, one time, there was a house party with some friends, and his dad picked him up, threw him in the air, and dropped him. He said he wasn't hurt, but everybody had a good laugh about it. He gives thanks for his work ethics and being a home owner to his dad.

Aunt Minnie was the sister of Momma who lived in Memphis, about an hour drive from us. She was the one who kept you laughing all the time. She did not take any stuff off of you. She married and had children.

In interviewing her eldest son, he spoke on how his mother would bring them out to the country in the summer. They would cross the old creek and go fishing over in the water area call Old Donny.

It would be his mom, my mom, and Aunt Viola and some of their children. They would catch some small fishes and take them back to our house and cook them. He said he enjoyed the fun in the country. He mentioned coming out and staying for a couple of weeks in the cold months after he had hip surgery.

He talked about how his mom told him about slavery time. She told him about when the lightning had struck a tree and that it would be gold in the old tree. One day, lightning did strike a tree down by the highway. His mom told him about it. She mentioned that there might be a pot of gold in the tree. He put on his boots and went down to the highway area and found the tree. He looked for that pot of gold. Well, he says he never did find it.

His mom would take them walking to the airport to see the airplanes to take off and land in the afternoons. They did not live too far from the airport.

Her son the football player, I called him. He played while in high school. He remembers his mom as loving to go fishing and visit her country side she loved so well. This was land that her dad had purchased. He remembers how they would come out to the country and take back pork meat from when my parents killed the hogs for the winter and good fresh canned goods filled with fruit and vegetables.

After their dad died, they would come out even more and enjoy the country. He recalls how the boys collected card boards and delivered newspapers to keep money coming in to help out in the house. This was after his dad's death, before she came back to live in her old house in the country. Now that Mom has passed, I now live in that same house.

Her youngest daughter said in her interview that she remembered her mother being at her happiest moment was when she was around her sisters and brothers and the time spent in the country. She grew up with some of her nieces and nephews. Her mom did not marry until later in life. She seemed as though, in this interview, she was glad that her mom had the opportunity to go back and live where she loved so much before her death.

My memories of Aunt Minnie were from when she and her family came out to our house from Memphis. We looked forward to it every time. I remember Aunt Minnie bringing out all those big bags of donuts when she came. Momma made dinner. We would have fried chicken, black-eyed peas, fried corn, corn bread, cool-aid, cakes, and pies.

Lynn would eat so much that he did not want his shirt to touch his stomach. The weather was hot, and he would be full. Lynn found a shade tree and leaned against it and looked as though he could barely breathe. Momma got such a kick out of him when he came to visit.

I can remember on a Sunday when they came to visit; one of her daughter's was learning how to drive. She got in Dad's old car. She put the car in drive, making loud noises with the gears, suddenly backed up then took off with full speed. She had so much dust flying that the dust made it to the house before she did. Everybody ran; this included Aunt Minnie, Momma, me, the dogs, and the cats.

Momma and Aunt Minnie were close and looked a lot alike. I got close to her after Momma died. She would still come down to visit with us. I was thirteen when Momma died, and, with her being there, it was company for me. I thought she made the best banana pudding.

Aunt Minnie made me a beautiful red dress by hand while sitting on our porch. I loved it. When I turned seventeen years old, she called me and told me to ask Daddy if I could take the bus to Memphis and go to the state fair. Daddy agreed.

I went on a Friday and returned home on Sunday. She had one son who later worked for the sheriff department. He would send Cody and me savings bonds from time to time. It meant so much to have them in our lives at such a difficult time.

<u>Aunt Lillie</u>, known as Aunt Lil, was Momma's youngest sister. She lived a walking distance up on the hill from us. She and her children were very close and close in age. We had plenty of fun.

Her eldest daughter remembered her mom in an interview with me as a mom who loved her church. She was a missionary and did a lot of traveling in the state of Tennessee and other states as well. Through many years of devoting herself to church work and traveling, she gained a lot of experience and knowledge about people.

When her mother became ill and could no longer get around like she used to, I came home to stay with her for a couple of weeks. One day, she was in the kitchen. Her mom called me to her bedside and said, "Minnie, in all my traveling, you know what I found out about these preachers? They ain't about saving souls; they are all about the money."

Her sons talked about how their mother would plan to whip the youngest son when he had done something wrong. Every time he was to get his whipping, he would run. The elder brother would say, "Momma, do you want me to catch him?" But when the elder brother tried to catch, the younger brother was too fast.

Their mom said, "That's all right. I'll get him." Sure enough, when he came in the house for the night she remembered. And whenever she whipped him outside, his dog, Floppy, would start growling and barking at Aunt Lil.

One of her daughters remembered how fascinated she was when she heard her mom say her ABCs backward and laughed about how her mom said if she married ever again, she would not marry a poor man.

Aunt Lil's youngest daughter and I were very close. She was saying that when they were in church, her mom would tell people when they give their testimony "Get up, reach high, strike fire, and sit down."

I recall my Aunt Lil as a person who was always at church. She married her husband, and he played the piano in church. She made the best pound cakes in town. I could eat her homemade vegetable soup every day.

She sold barbecue sandwiches in town. She set up a stand along the alley, and when we went to church, I can recall how we would get on the morning bench for prayer. We were there for our sins and to get saved. Yes, we went to that bench several times.

When the adults came around, my two cousins told me, "Just say, I want prayer." The only problem was, I couldn't half hear because the music and people were so loud, praising the Lord.

So when the adults came around and asked me, "What do you want?" I said, "I want pray."

I don't think they heard me because they kept right on singing and praying. This is probably why I could never get saved from my sins and had to stay on the morning bench. Of course, my daddy told me it was a difference in saying a prayer and just praying.

Uncle James was Momma's youngest brother. He also became a minister later on in life. He and his second wife Ruby also had a daycare there at their church.

His children, a son and a daughter, remember their dad as playful and loving. The daughter told me in her interview, how their dad would take them to Sunday school. They used to ride in his tow truck from his job. They lived in Washington at the time. He was the only African American mechanic located in Washington, DC and attended mechanic school.

When he got his first car, he gave them boogie rides. She remembers it as being a 1955 blue-and-white Ford. Boogie rides are when you put one foot on the gas and the other on the brake and rotate each movement. This would make the car rock like a rocking horse. What fun they had!

She told me that when they played hide and seek, he would get involved. As she was the youngest her brother would try to find her. Her dad would pick her up and put her on the top shelf in the closet so her brother could not find her. She remembers how her dad would drive their mom over to her friend's house on Sunday afternoons.

Uncle James used to come out to the country where we lived. He married his first wife and had two children. I cannot remember his first wife. I was just a little girl when she died.

This wife told me the story of how he used to ask her when they were in school and when she was going to get rid of her pig tails in her hair. She and his first wife were good friends while in school. When Uncle James went into the service, he later married her friend.

Uncle James talked about women coming through the front door, backdoor, side door, and the window after his first wife died. He decided he needed someone in his life. He had been asking about his wife now. He somehow ended up with her telephone number and had it on the mantle there in his living room.

His wife now, lived and work as a beautician in Detroit. He picked up the telephone number and called her. They talked, and he ended up with her as his wife.

I remember how they would come home together before they decided to move back home years later. During the summer months, I recall his children coming out to stay a few weeks with us. Uncle was alone and had to work.

His daughter was afraid of bugs. I figured that they were probably afraid of us too. We were looking pretty bad. But it did not matter to us. We loved and enjoyed them whenever they came.

Once I became grown, married, and with children, I visited my uncle and aunt. He always wanted me to make him a cheesecake. He called it "cherry pie."

He had an appetite out of this world. He cut half of the cheesecake and put in a large plate, with the other half of the plate with vanilla ice cream, and topped it off with a big glass of milk. He reminded me of his father, Grandpa West.

In Memory of
my brothers and Sister

Columbus

WHEN MY ELDEST BROTHER Columbus was living at home, I was not born yet. Therefore, I did not learn much about him until I moved to Michigan where he lived. Most of my knowledge of him came from my elder brothers and sisters.

I do know that he had such a smooth cool walk. Clinora says she thought he had a Danzel Washington walk. He was very soft spoken and kindhearted. He and his friend were the best checker and card players on this side of Texas.

I was told that he once had driven to Bolivar from Michigan alone. When he was driving back, he picked up a hitchhiker. He let the hitch hiker drive while he took a nap in the back seat of his car.

From my interviews with his children, they had a lot of fun with him. He was a prankster! One of his daughters was sixteen and was trying to sneak a smoke in her upstairs bedroom. Columbus, her dad, took the water hose and sprayed water into the bedroom window. The cigarette was wet, and so was she. She talked about how he took a raccoon and chased them through the house with it.

His son tells how his dad owned a gun. It was so old that when he pulled it out to show him how the gun worked, it fell apart in his hands.

His other daughter talked about how she had a car. She had driven the wheels practically off of it. She needed some repairs done to her car, so she told her dad. He kindly told her with his soft voice to wait until morning.

The next morning, when she got out of bed, he told her to pull the car around back. She did exactly what he told her to do after she had gotten dressed. She pulled the car up. She noticed a pitcher of water, a glass, a chair, and his tools.

She started to sit in the chair. He told her, "Wait a minute. If you need your car repaired, I'll show you." He gave her hands-on training, and, later, she and her dad worked on each other's cars from time to time. She now owns two repair shops.

In my interview with my brother-West, he told me that when he was a little boy, he remembers Columbus leaving home at age thirteen. He went to Humboldt, Tennessee. He got a job in a fertilizer place. He was fourteen years old when he moved to Michigan where he found a job. He moved in with our father's cousin. This is where he met his wife Maple.

According to Ethel Columbus was a trapper of animals. He would catch and sell the furs. And Allie said he not only caught animals, but he also caught her in one of his traps. Mom came down and got her out of the trap.

James told me in an interview how Columbus was going to show him the city when he first came to Michigan. Columbus went into the bathroom to shave while he sat in the living room dressed and ready to go. After a while, he came out, and he had shaved half of his mustache off. Columbus told him, he so often called people, "Well, "Bub," we wouldn't be going out tonight." He not only did not go out on the town, but he also did not go anyplace else.

Carl still remembers Columbus as calling him "Bub."

His wife Maple told how Columbus had put some money in the bank. Since he did not trust the bank, he and his friend went to a field and watched the bank because he thought someone was going to rob it while his money was in it.

Columbus was the first born to momma and daddy. He led a way for all the siblings. We all ended in Detroit at some point in time. We never know when we set out to do things in our lives whether or not it will have an impact on someone else.

Idell

Idell was the eldest sister and the first girl to leave home. She joined Columbus in Michigan. She started to work and married with two daughters. They spoke of how good she was and how she pushed education on a daily basis. She loved to travel and dress. They admired her very much. She was always available not only to them for advice but to her neighbors and their friends as well.

My older siblings told me how she paid for a water well to be dug for Momma and Daddy when she went back home to visit. She brought back sisters and sister-in-laws to live in Michigan. She had three sisters to live with her for a while but not all at the same time.

Eunice told how Idell was in labor with her last child. She acted as a midwife helping to deliver her baby. She lived with Idell when she first came to Detroit. Matter of fact, Idell got her a job where she was employed. She lived with her until she met and married her husband. They had fun together.

Allie talked about how protective she was over her younger sisters. They spent a lot of time together. They went out and had some of the same friends. She lived with Idell until she met and married her husband. Idell had her eldest daughter, and Allie had her son during the same year.

Ethel says Idell loved children and would help anyone who needed help. When she lived in the south, in order for her to go to high school, she had to live near town with an older couple. When Ethel first came to Detroit, she lived with Idell and babysat her two children so Idell could work. She lived with Idell until she met and married her husband.

She put on a reception in her backyard for Clinora and her husband when they married. She loved to bowl. We did not spend a lot of time together. She wished that she could have gotten to know her better and spent more time together, says Clinora

I can recall how Idell would drive all the way to Tennessee and back to Detroit. I thought she was the most driving woman I knew. We would always be glad to see her. We loved hearing about Detroit.

After Momma died, I can remember how Idell would buy her daughters back-to-school clothes; but she would buy mine as well. When I was going to the eleventh grade, I took up typing for the first time. Idell sent me a blue typewriter for a gift. My typing speed improved thanks to her. I did not ask for it she just sent it out of the goodness of her heart.

I guess with Momma dying at my age of thirteen, Idell knew that Daddy did not know much about buying clothes for a girl. She also knew that he did not have the money. With Idell buying the clothes, I was able to look pretty good when school started. I certainly appreciated that.

She had a big heart on giving and helping others. And the good part was she was like Momma—no charge for her love. I do know she loved her girls dearly, and I will never forget what she did for me.

Idell had her eldest daughter in the same year Momma had me, her youngest daughter. I can think back to when she drove down to Tennessee to pick Momma and me up. She also drove us over to Cleveland during the summer months.

After Momma's death, I would go to Detroit and stay with Idell. She made sure I ate well and had clothes and fun. I can remember her taking her daughters, their friends, and me to the amusement parks and how we all would be sitting on the porch and wait for the ice cream truck.

When Regina, her eldest daughter, was about sixteen years old, she would take me to parties where her friends were. When Idell said be back home a certain time, she meant it. We had to be inside the door and not a minute later. After I graduated and came to Detroit to live, she gave me one of her cars.

When Idell was ill in the hospital, I heard about it the night before. The next day, I went straight to the hospital from work. I walked into the hospital, and they asked if they could help me. I gave them my sister's name, and they directed me to where she was.

The nurses made me stand in the hallway for a few minutes. The door was wide open; therefore, I could see directly into the recovery room. They wheeled her out. I stood there like the nurse told me to do.

Idell turned her head in the direction of me and waved her hand motioning for me to come into the room. The nurse gave me the okay. As I entered the room, Idell grabbed my hand. She started talking so fast. I did not know what to make of it because I had not ever seen her this way before.

She told me, "Girl, I was dying. I was drifting away, and I heard a song. It was such a sweet song." She went on to say, "I didn't feel sick anymore. It was so peaceful. When you go, I want you to go that same way."

With white foam built up around each corner of her mouth while she continued to talk, she said, "I told the doctors that

I knew they had done all they could. I know they thought I was crazy. But I was trying to tell the story, and I couldn't tell it fast enough. Tell Clinora to come down here and write my testimony."

Some days later, Idell died from her illness.

Idell was the second eldest and the eldest daughter to be born to my momma and daddy. She told her story. It was written by Clinora. This was a woman that touched the lives of many in more ways than one. The bible teaches us, the measure you give, the measure you get back. She showed and shared her love and the love was returned by many. Who knows, if it wasn't for her, I might not be writing today.

Arthur

My brother Arthur left home when I was three years old. He returned when I was nine years old. He was the quiet type. He had a contagious laugh. Even when his jokes weren't that funny, his laugh would get you every time.

His children talked about how he would have a coon in the freezer in the basement. They were afraid to go get ice cream out of the freezer because they thought they had killed the dog. They spoke on how he was there for them for their weddings and their illnesses.

Allie remembers the time she called Arthur to tell him about a mutual friend of theirs. The friend was in the hospital and wasn't doing well. She continued on with her conversation stating what the doctor said about the friend's illness when suddenly Arthur interrupts her with; "well when is the funeral". Also, after he was grown and with a family, he had gone to his doctor for a visit. He visited Allie at her home. When he walked in and sat down, he begin with, well I went to the doctor today. He said at some point my rib had been broken. Allie replied; what! Looking over at her he says; yea you probably dropped me as a baby and broke my ribs. And they both laughed. She misses his visits and conversations they had.

Ethel remembers him giving her, her very first car. She also talked about how he used to frighten her with a dead snake when they were growing up.

Eunice said she recalls how he drove all the way from Detroit to Cleveland and stayed one hour at her house and drove back to Detroit.

James remembered the time he and Arthur went out to a house party. He says that Arthur would always try to get the prettiest girl every time. This particular night, he got the prettiest girl. But he has always had two left feet when it came to dancing.

James says he thought maybe the woman had bad feet already. He kept stepping on the lady's feet. She finally said, "I've heard of people who can't dance, but *you*, you are ridiculous," and she left the party.

Clinora remembers most that he would help her with her children sometimes when she went to work and his eating habits and that one-of-a-kind laugh. She said it went like this, "Uh-huh-huh-uh-huh-huh-UN-huh-h-h-h-!"

Arthur used to ask Cody why you work for one Big Three plant and drive a different Big Three vehicle. And when he had the bible in his hands, Arthur would say, "Hey, Cody! What are you doing carrying that bible in your hand?" And he would start that one of a kind laugh.

Carl remembers Arthur as a man of a few words. He was a one-liner guy. He said what he had to say in such short sentences. He would come by and pick him up, and they would enjoy telling old stories.

He told me how Momma used to whip Arthur for something that he had done for some kind of foolishness. Arthur had a dog. Every time Momma would try to whip him, the dog would tear at her stockings.

I can remember Momma introducing me to my brother Arthur. How can I forget a brother that replaced sugar with salt for my biscuit sandwich.

Coming to Detroit for the summer from Bolivar, I had fun and some surprises. When I was about sixteen years old, he picked me up from my sister Idell's house and took me over to my sister Ethel's house.

He had a drunken friend in the backseat of his car. His car had those bucket seats in it. I remember having on a pair of hip-hugger pants and a short top at the time. It was the style then.

We were approaching the traffic light. His friend ran his hand just underneath my blouse. I raised my voice, "Stop!" Arthur hit the brakes under the light and said, "If you don't take your hands off my baby sister, I will kick your blank, blank, blank.

Talk about "*shocked*"; I was. If you knew him the way most of us did, you would have done just what the man and I did. I did not turn my head to look at Arthur. And I was afraid to even cut my eyes to look over at him. I froze.

I did not hear the man say anything in the backseat. I did not know if he had stopped breathing or not. And I did not care at this point. I just knew, as long as I could survive this ride and still be breathing, I wasn't going to worry about the man or anything else.

When I arrived at Ethel's house, the man did not say anything as I exited the car, and I did not either. I did not even look back. I was like the woman in the bible; he (Arthur) might turn me into a pillar of salt. I ran into the house. I took no chance with him. I loved him dearly and am thankful for all his love and protection.

Arthur was the seventh child to be born to momma and daddy. We never know who will love and protect us in the time of need. It is never too late to learn that the lesson you learn will be better for you in the long run. It is called tough love. It may sound harsh at the time but turns out it is not as bad as it seems. Tough love is something sometimes we should learn to appreciate.

Freddie

Freddie's children spoke of how they remembered their daddy as one of the strongest men they knew. The boys remembered how he took them fishing and hunting. The time he spent with them, they appreciated it. His daughters recalled how protective he was over them.

Allie remembered all the coffee they shared together because Freddie was her weekly visitor. She spoke of him being the comedian in the family.

Ethel remembers him more as a little fellow because they used to go fishing together back home. Also, how James, Carl, Carnell, and Freddie would go back home and hunt every November.

Clinora and Freddie were closer in age. She recalls him as being the brother that would be the one that got the two of them rides home when they were out on dates. He would tell his younger sisters and brothers, "Let me taste your food. I'm not ready to eat mine yet. Let me see if yours going to taste any different than mine."

She thought back to when her finger was cut by him. It was not on purpose. They were young and she recalls how afraid he was.

Carl remembered Freddie saying, "Don't worry about the mule; just load the wagon." It did not matter what type of work they were doing. He thought back to how they went home together every year in November to hunt. Carl says he was the cook out of the bunch. Maybe it had to do with him being a cook in the service. Freddie was one of the biggest eaters. They were close and had loads of fun together.

At the time I was growing up, I can start remembering Freddie on down to my age. Freddie grew up in the house with us. Freddie was definitely known for his phrase, "Let, let, let, let me taste yours." And he would say it fast, as if he had some type of speech impairment. "Let me see if yours taste like mine," he would say. It did not matter whether it was a coke or a cracker. He would always pull that on the younger ones under him.

As I think back when Momma was still living, at the time, Freddie and Daddy had gone to cut fire wood. Momma was in the kitchen cooking. I was looking for something in the dresser drawers. I ran across this big beautiful shinny something. I just couldn't pass it up.

Right away I had dreams for it. It was a nice fifty cent piece. I peeped to see if Momma was near the door. I got the fifty cent and took it outside. I rubbed it in the dirt. I tried scratching it up real good, and make it look old and dirty.

I ran into the house and called to Momma, "I found a fifty cent piece." Momma never looked up and she never stopped mixing up the corn bread. She said so very calmly, "Gal, put that boy's money back in that drawer."

I knew I didn't have a choice. Because if I did not, I would have been wearing that corn bread before it hit the baking pan.

I recall Momma and Daddy being so very proud of Freddie in his cap and gown. He graduated from Allen White High School, and it was held at night. By the last name being Weaver, that put him at the end. I fell asleep before he came up on stage to get his diploma.

Momma said, "You missed your brother getting his diploma." They were some proud parents that night. Freddie was a lot of fun with his twisted smile. He was a free hearted brother and will always be missed.

Freddie was the ninth child to be born to momma and daddy. Love can be displayed in many ways. It does not always have to be serious. Love can be fun as well. We always worry about many things that we cannot change. We can load up problems that we do not have to have. But, why worry about it. God will not put any more on you than you can bear.

Carnell

Carnell's daughters remembered their Dad as funny and one who loved old songs. He would get up in the mornings and make them breakfast. He took them riding at night to the park playing those old songs and site seeing.

They recalled how he told them they did not have to wear makeup to try and look beautiful because they had that natural beauty like their mom. They did not have to seek attention from men to validate their beauty. They spoke of how much they appreciated him.

His son recalled how his dad would take him on some of his jobs. Carnell use to be a repair man for a well-known company. He could repair almost anything. His son said his dad would pay him. He encouraged him to save his money. And if he had to invest in anything with his money, invest in tools. The tools would make money for him.

He also remembered how, one time, his dog had stopped breathing in the backyard, and he called his dad. Carnell gave his dog CPR. Even though the dog did not make it, it was the special effort he put into caring for this animal.

Our sister Allie described Carnell as one with those story-telling eyes. If he did not approve of what you are saying in your conversation with him, his eyes would say so, without him speaking a word. Carnell had to be introduced to Allie because of the age difference. Allie had left home when he was born.

Our sister Ethel remembered when he was born. She recalled him as being about a ten-pound baby. Everyone was talking about how big of a baby he was. She talked about how he remembered her house when he came back from the service. She could not understand how he remembered her house and not anyone else's since he had never lived with her.

He worked with our elder brother James from time to time. James owned his own plumbing business outside of working his regular job. He told me that Carnell could repair anything that was before him. And even though it was a few brothers and a sister in between their age, they became closer by spending time together while working.

Carnell and Carl were close in age. Carl told me how much fun he and Carnell had growing up. As children, they would do things and get into trouble. He remembered, one time, they were in the fields. They were putting down fertilizer for the crops. The wind was kind of high. Daddy knew that the wind would blow the fertilizer all over the field.

Carnell was rather tall. So he told Carnell to bend down because the wind was blowing too high. Carnell waited until Daddy got past him with the mule and stood up and continued to throw the fertilizer.

When he heard Daddy say, "Woe, stop, mule," they knew he was in trouble. Carnell told Carl, "I knew I had messed up." So he froze and couldn't run. That's one time he learned that a hard head makes a soft behind.

Carl also remembers how they served in the arm forces at the same time. He received a telephone call from him. He told Carl this army business is not playing. They thought that the work Daddy gave them did not compare to what was expected from Uncle Sam.

Clinora recalled, when we were growing up, how talented Carnell was. One time, our old wringer washer had broken. He repaired the washing machine. She liked cooking, and Carnell would always come into the kitchen to pick on her until, one day, he came in the kitchen without a shirt on. He took some food and started running out the backdoor. She took some hot home-made mashed potatoes on a fork and threw them on his back. She knows now that it was cruel thing to do that to him.

She thought back to when he wrecked Daddy's car one night. He lost control. The next day, they had the car pulled out of a ditch. He was okay, and so was the car.

Cody remembers how he and Carnell were close growing up. They worked in the fields together. And, after Carnell went into the service, he would come by and pick him up. He said they did some foolish things together when they were growing up. He remembers the coon, squirrel, rabbit hunting, and the fishing.

Carnell (Boot, we called him), he clowned around a lot. He liked to have fun and make you laugh. I remember one Sunday afternoon, Momma and Daddy had gone to church. Aunt Lillie and Uncle Preston had gone to church as well. My two cousins, Ruthie and Ruby, and I, had gone from their house to our house several times. We really should have been in church with our parents. But they trusted the elder brothers to watch over us.

Carnell was down in the woods hunting. Their brother Charles was someplace else. You'll find out later where he was.

Well, after we were going back and forth so much, I guess we got bored. We ate the last piece of corn bread at my house. We had just left our house and were halfway to my cousin's house when Carnell yelled, "Y'all ate the last piece of corn bread," and a gun shot went off. One of us said, "uh-oh!" He had shot up in the air.

Naturally, we started running and, may I add, fast! We thought he was shooting at us. We were so out of breath when we made that turn to go up the hill to their house. By this time, we were jogging at a slow pace.

All of a sudden, here came Charles, their brother. He was out of breath as well, jogging alongside of us. He asked, "Did y'all hear that gun shot?" I looked over at him since he was right next to me. He was out of breath too.

He had run so fast that he still had watermelon juice dangling from his chin. It did not have time to dry. And watermelon seeds were still stuck to his shirt. You see, he was up in our neighbor's watermelon patch across the barbed-wire fence. I guess, he thought the man was shooting at him.

I knew when we were in school, Carnell used to love the army pictures that used to come on television. One was called 12 O'clock High, and the other was Combat. He later joined the army.

I can remember how he would pick at me so much, and I would chase him with rocks. I threw them, but I was afraid to really hit him. I knew that if I did hit him, I had two whippings coming. One would have been from him and the other from Momma.

One time, Momma was saying something was stealing her eggs out of the hen house. Carnell said, "I'll find out for you, Momma. I'll catch him." Sure enough, he found out. It was an old chicken snake headed for the chicken house late in the evening.

He caught the snake. He picked it up with one hand at the back of its head and the other hand at its tail. Being the brother that he was, he told us to go get some fire. I ran like a fool and got some fire.

He said, "I am going to see if snakes really have feet and legs." And I, as a young girl, watched closely. No, I did not see feet and legs. He went on and killed the snake. We did have a lot of fun moments together. I've missed those special days and him.

Before Carnell died, he was eager to go home with his elder brothers when they were in Tennessee during the hunting season in November. This was the year before he died. He had his bag in his hand sitting on the porch, waiting for them to come by to pick him up.

He waited for a while and began to think that they were not coming to pick him up. He dug up a flower or two from his backyard to take with him. You see, he was not going home to go hunting at all. He was going to visit and plant flowers on Momma and Daddy's graves in the country cemetery. He died a few months later. This was the kind of heart he had.

Carnell was the twelfth child and youngest son to be born to momma and daddy. We all should be so lucky to display love and compassion for love ones. Have you ever heard the song give me my flowers while I am living then my living would not have been in vain? It is never too late to give your flowers. It does not matter how they are displayed in life. It could be a kind gesture as Carnell had.

It seems as though there aren't any values when it comes to one's life nowadays. It is as if a person or the life of that person doesn't even exist. We not only take the life of others for granted, but we sometimes tend to take our own life for granted. It is then, when illness strikes us, that we began to appreciate life.

We treat each other as if the next person does not have feelings. It amazes me when I see people who continually push and take advantage of the next person. It does not matter if it is a loved one or a coworker or boss on the job. We never know what the next person has gone through or are going through.

Our own feelings seem to outweigh the respect and consideration of others. Let me give you an example. I have a friend who was going through some things not only at home, but also on the job. This friend fell ill. All the unconcerned people who surrounded them wanted to be concerned after their illness.

I think this concern was needed more before their illness. When you have not done all you know you could have done for that person, it is not a very good feeling when this person sees you. The sad part about this is that the people who are contributing to the problem carry on as if they have not done anything wrong.

And what do we do? We continue with the same old ways and the same old attitude until, one day, illness hits us. Where are the respect and the value of one's life?

When you hear the stories and testimonies of people who have gone through illnesses, you feel bad for them. You pray for them. But you do not have the faintest idea how and what they have gone and are going through.

It does not matter whether it is cancer, aids, stroke, or diabetes, etc. The struggles and hardship that they endure must be something that for one moment, if they could let you feel what they are feeling, we may be able to understand. A moment of relief for that person would be something that probably can be felt for a lifetime.

Take a look at many cases where people are ill. They do not choose to be ill or choose their illnesses. There are accidents that happen; we do not always choose that accident. What do we do? We feel bad for the person it happened to, but we continue on with the same attitude and, in some cases, the same consideration. I learned in life that the best recipe for a bad attitude is to have a good attitude.

After the death of so many family members and friends, I have started looking at life differently. Maybe getting older plays a part in this outlook. But I feel good about looking at life in a positive way. I feel good that I can care about the next person and the next person's feelings. I feel good that I do not have to take advantage of the next person. All of us at some point in life have known something good about someone else. And someone else has known something good about us. You know what! We should treat each other in such a way that it will make a difference in each other's lives.

Why not? What if it was me? Wouldn't it be nice to always keep in mind, that when life is over for your loved ones that you can honestly know that you have done everything in your power that you could possibly do for them?

This is in my opinion and views only. The contents in this section *do not exclude me*. I would like to put forth an effort to share this information with you. I should hope you will accept this in a positive way.

Words

When we are choosing our words, we should be very careful how we choose them. Sometimes, words can be just as painful as being on punishment. We need to be careful in what we say to each other and about each other. Words can hurt. It is so easy to destroy someone else's life with just a couple of negative words. The tongue can be just as powerful as a sharp knife.

We all know how it feels to be hurt by someone else's words. We should be so very careful before we speak.

Forgive

How can we expect God to forgive us if we are not willing to forgive each other? Wesley B. believed in peace, and so does God. As they say, "Let go, and let God." We must move on with our lives with a positive outlook because tomorrow is not promised.

Take a look at the illnesses, accidents, murders, and wars, etc. There is enough bad baggage; why carry on that extra weight that you do not have to have? Time will bring about a change. Why not lighten the load?

Wesley B. said, "In due time." She meant "keep on living and you will see what I mean." If someone has done well in your life, let them know. If they have not, do not dwell on it; move on. Another Wesley B.'s quotes: "Even a fool can't argue by himself."

When we make a choice in our lives, it is the choice that we have made. We will have to be the one to live with that choice. Let's just hope they are good positive choices. We cannot live someone else's life. Sometimes, it gets pretty hard trying to live our own.

You never know what the next person has gone through or is currently going through. They may not discuss it with you, but it doesn't mean that they are not going through something. Maybe they have chosen one person to discuss their problem with. It may not be to slight you in anyway. Or maybe they are talking to God about it. Do not be so quick to judge. Here we go, the bible says, "Judge not, that ye not be judged" Mathew 7:1.

Gossip

Have you ever been in such a deep thought and someone passes you and you did not speak? You later learn that they said you are stuck up. Or a big deal is made out of it. Most likely, it wasn't to ignore them. Maybe you just had a lot on your mind at the time.

And when you hear part of a story, please do not draw conclusions. When you hear all of a story, do not draw conclusions because whomever you heard that story from may not have all the facts. One word like is or was can make a difference. There goes someone's reputation.

Here we go again the bible says; whoso keepeth his mouth and his tongue keepth his soul from troubles. Proverbs 21: 23

We know that we build up trash in our garbage cans. What do we do? When it gets full, we get rid of it and take it out. That's the way our lives should be. Throw away unneeded trash. Put in a new liner in your life and start fresh.

Be careful what you keep. By getting rid of the trash, you will find that you will not feel so heavily burdened and possibly feel much lighter. The lighter the load, the easier it is to carry it. Peel off stress, troubles, and confusion.

According to Proverbs 11:13, "A talebearer revealeth secrets: but he that is of a faithful spirit concealeth the matter." (Whoever comes to you with gossip may also be a person who will gossip about you.)

Strangers

As an adult, we teach our children to stay away from strangers. It is a good idea. It can be very harmful to them. And it can be very devastating for family members.

We see all the rapes, disappearances of children and adults, and even death. But when we are in the stores, church, at work, or just passing by, we should be careful how we treat people in general.

Yes, with the way things are today, you are subject to get cursed at, threatened, etc. But how do we know whether or not it is not one of God's angels? Maybe he or she does not have to have those visible wings we read about. We never know who God has sent to help or protect us.

Have you ever wondered why you weren't hit by that moving car that just missed you or that box that fell off the shelf? All we say is "Thank God."

Think about it; you could have gotten hit, but you didn't. Life is too short. We do not have to live with a lot of unnecessary, ungrateful challenges in our lives. Most of the time, we just choose to. Again, Wesley B. would say tomorrow is not promised and don't go to bed angry because tomorrow may be too late to say I'm sorry.

Parenting

Are there any perfect parents now or in the past? Since the bible teaches us none is perfect but God, I guess that means no. We are taught by our parents on how to be a parent. We pick up many of their habits and teachings as they have picked up from their parents.

We often say I am going to raise my children differently. I do not want them to have to go through what I went through. Please know that being a parent is often self-taught. It is simply because each child or each spouse is different from your siblings.

You may have told yourself, "I want my parenting to be like my neighbor's or a particular celebrity." The surface may look good, but living in that household could be worse than the household you are living in. Have you ever heard the expressions on the outside looking in? Everything glittering is not gold. Please do not be fooled without knowing the facts.

Learned behavior can be negative, or it can be positive. Know that if you want to be different from the way your parents raised you, then be determined to work on it, practice it, and stay in prayer.

Sometimes, no matter how much you say, "I'm not going to be like Momma or Daddy." Some parts of your parent's behavior and features are inherited. They could have died and could have not been in your life before you were born. But please know; there will be something about them that will be in you.

Choose the positive roads as far as behavior. You cannot do anything about the looks, unless you decide to have plastic surgery. Then what about your mannerism or your walk? Accept what God has given you. He has given you five senses. We should use them to the best of our ability in a positive way.

Your children are looking up to you before entering the schools or the streets. Remember, they are our future. What examples are we setting for them? How can we tell them to do something that we are not willing to do ourselves?

There is a future for all of us. We have to be determined to do well so we can see it. Do not sit back and say, "Well, let someone else do it." Be productive. Life is a challenge. And so is parenting and growing up as a child.

Do not be a person who says, "I am going to do this and keep putting it off." If you plan to do it, plan it, and act on it. Please do not be one of those I'm-going-to-do people and never get started or even finish. Be known by your planning and finishing your goal. Do not let your finish line be an unaccomplished goal before your death. What is your goal?

Anger

Who does not get angry? Release and let go of it! It is not good for you, your surroundings, or the person you are attacking. Many times, we are not really angry with the next person. We are angry with ourselves and take it out on the next person.

There have been times that we have been angry and worked up over something we have heard somebody say. It is best sometimes if we did not hear it. We should be careful about getting worked up over it and be careful not to act on it.

Look at children, how they fight over things. Sometimes, it is not things that were theirs in the first place. This is the way adults are as well. We fight over things that we did not pay a dime for.

If someone gives you something, appreciate it. Try to realize God gave you something with no charge to you, as he has given life and his love. Just think he can take away what he has given you, including your life in a blink of an eye.

We have been upset over things on television and have lost friendships over it. The person on television does not know you personally or know you even exist. The ones who are arguing have lost friendship. The person on television will still be making their money and you have lost your best friend.

One may end up with a stroke and the other with a heart attack. Think about it; nothing positive will become of it and, nine times out of ten, nothing is accomplished really. We need to let go. Do you want to live the rest of your life stressed and upset when you do not have to?

Judging

Yes, I mentioned before about the scripture in Mathew 7:1. How many of us have been judging others and get upset when we get judged? That's rather selfish isn't it? But we all are pretty much guilty of it.

Will it stop us?—probably not. Of course, we can practice on improving it on a daily basis. Just because someone else is doing it, does not mean we have to.

Being judged and not know it is one thing, but to be judged and know it is another. I think the worst is to be judged in the face of the person that is doing the judging. That can be a painful and dangerous thing.

Consider how you would feel if you were in their shoes at that time. If you are angry when you are doing the judging, you probably will not care that you are hurting the next person. And if you have that don't-care attitude, you probably will not let it enter your mind.

However, it should because it might be you the next time in their shoes, maybe not by the same person but someone else. We should think before we speak and act. I heard once, "Never say anything bad about a man until you've walked a mile in his shoes." Who knows by the time he is miles away, even though you can talk about him, Guess what? He cannot hear you. We should think before we speak and act.

Complaining

We should be grateful that we are alive, well, and able to complain. But why should we complain everyday about everything and everybody? If we think about it, we will not be the only one complaining. The world does not have just you in it. And God did not put only you here on this earth.

A lot of times, complaining just becomes a habit. It somehow brings satisfaction to the complainer and not to the person they are complaining about. Try telling that complainer that they must be awfully unhappy. He or she will easily say, "Oh no, I'm happy with myself." But are they really?

It cannot be that everybody in this world is wrong about every problem you have with them. Could it be that the complainer is the one with the problem? We may need to search our own minds and hearts.

Do you want the best, or do you want to stand back and admire someone else's best? There is a price for everything in this world. Do not just admire the best; get and be the best you can be. Always remember, no one is better than you!

Family and friends can have a knock-out fight. But nobody else can say anything about them. Therefore, the knock-out fight is not worth having. Have you ever loved your favorite record and, at some point, you got tired of it? That is the way people are.

The old saying is "You sound like a broken record." Well, we can turn the record off for a while to get away from it. This does not mean that the record is still not your favorite. Sometimes, in life, we need to step away from some problems, people, and things, and regroup.

Wesley B. would say, "For peace's sake." Time moves on, and so can love. Keep this in mind.

Just because the person that's not doing the complaining is not complaining along with the complainer, does not mean that the non-complainer can't out-complain the complainer. Have you ever thought that the non-complainer feels it's just not worth it?

Some people complain about living alone and being alone. In some cases, in order not to be alone, you must get alone with others. Sometimes we are so unhappy that we cannot stand ourselves. If you stand alone, you will be alone.

If I were you

We all have a habit of saying, "If I were you, I would do it this way or that way." "If you were me, then you would be me, and you would be doing exactly what I am doing," Says my eldest brother-West.

He has a point. How can we become someone else? We have our own body, mind, thoughts, feelings, and plans. We do according to our will and not someone else's. It is a full-time job taking care of ourselves and our household and surroundings.

We have the tendency to run the lives of the other person. When we spend so much time running the next person's life; something or somebody will most likely go lacking.

Plan according to the way your body feels and the way your mind thinks. There is no one in this world who can tell you how good or bad your body feels. This includes the doctors. They have studied and can imagine how you must feel. But each person and each body might experience a different feeling. You might be able to take the flu shot. I may not be able to take the flu shot. Since I cannot be you I guess I have to remain myself.

We all should be careful in what and how we say things to one another, not that we mean any harm when we phrase it. As the younger generation put it, "It's all good!" And a little older generation would say, "No skin off my back! And check yourself!"

Time

Spend your time wisely because you will never know when it is your last hour. Have you ever lost a family member, friend, neighbor, or a coworker, and you get the news they are gone? One of the first things we say is "I just saw them," or "I just talked to them."

Time is very important. Let's not waste it on foolishness. Look around you and just know who you are leaving behind.

We should be careful of what we do in life. Children look at everything we do. Examples need to be set. Mistakes are going to be made. But that time can be used to correct these mistakes.

Think of the sacrifice our parents made for us. Time and love is the best gift you can give a child. Let us not say we got to get our groove on, or the children just have to wait. Well, a very good thought should have been put into that before getting the children. It sounds like we got our groove on, the reason we had the children in the first place. Make some sacrifices for your children. *They are worth it.*

Abuse

As you know and can imagine, there are several types of abuse. Without naming the different forms of abuse, let's just think on the way abuse can take place. This includes abuse to someone else physically or mentally. What about abuse to yourself?

What about the people who have lost their lives? They are gone. But look at the pain they left behind. All of their family members, neighbors, and friends are suffering from the hurt and pain.

What about the little children? Have parents really looked into their children's eyes and imagine what their little hearts could take if something should happen to them? If we think more about the helpless children, maybe we will not have such selfish love.

My sister Allen once said, "Some people do not choose the way they want to die. On the other hand, there are some who choose the way they want to die."

People do not choose cancer. But they do choose other ways of dying. We all have a choice to make; let us make the right choice. We should choose wisely and carefully. As long as I am in my right mind and able to make my own choices, I would rather not have someone else or something run or ruin my life's choices. How about you?

Promises

Why put off today because you think you will be able to do tomorrow. Tomorrow is not promised, why wait? You might go to get up and can't. And when tomorrow comes, something else may come up.

I can recall my sister Clinora was learning a poem for school. She was in high school at the time. She went on and on with tomorrow, tomorrow, and tomorrow. She got stuck for so long on tomorrow, tomorrow, and tomorrow until Daddy stood up from his chair and said, "I show will be glad when tomorrow gets here." He walked out of the house.

So remember not to keep repeating and planning for tomorrow simply because tomorrow will continue to come, but you might not be here or be able to say or see tomorrow. There will always be a tomorrow, but will you be in that tomorrow? And would you have finished your promises?

Bond

You can look at bond in more than one way. As mentioned before, Daddy would say, "Your word is your bond." This means you can be trusted if you give your word. But if you lie, this mean you cannot be trusted. He was known for his word. He was respected and trusted in his community as his parents, Marion and Anna Weaver.

We can also bond together as a family by communicating, keeping the peace among ourselves, helping each other, and keeping prayer and God in our lives and our surroundings. You do not have to find God just in the church; it can be found in you. Think about it; you can't bring home the church building, but you can bring home the word.

Don't get me wrong; by all means, go to church. But when you leave the church, make sure you continue your word through your actions. You can go to church and learn nothing and continue to be the same way you were coming out as you were going in.

Making an impression and pleasing man should not be your concern. Keep pleasing God should be our concern. Look at the sick and shut-ins we have. They can have as much church and love for God in them as one that goes every day. Remember, only God knows your heart. Why should we be so judgmental?

Blame

"It's your fault." How many times have we heard that? "If it wasn't for her or him, I would have turned out differently." This may be true to a certain degree. But how about when you get grown and can learn for yourself how life should and could be?

If your life is not to your liking, you have a chance to do something about it. There is room for changes in your life for the better. Only you and God can make that change and improvement.

Now, the blame needs to stop because you can do something about it. If the person you are blaming dies, what are you going to do? Well, you will have to do what you have to do to make it for yourself.

Why not start now? Take the blame out of your complaining and do better. Think about this, the dead person is just that, dead. He or she does not know that you are blaming him or her. You continue to get yourself all worked up—for whose sake?

Don't quit

Whatever dreams you may have, make sure you follow it. If you get sidetracked, go back and pick up where you left off. Do not just plan and think about it. Be true to yourself, and live your dreams to the fullest. God gave you your life. Please be productive with it.

Children are guided, taught, and prayed for. Hopefully, whatever they learned from it will be positive for their future. And parents need to stop blaming the children because they think the children are holding them back.

According to Joshua 1:9; "Have not I commanded thee? Be strong and of a good courage; be not afraid, neither be thou dismayed: for the Lord thy God is with thee whithersoever thou go-est." Do not get confused with your wishbone and your backbone. You can wish all day and do nothing and have nothing, but a backbone seems to get the job done.

Sin

We all have sinned. It doesn't matter how you try to dice it, slice it, or dress it up to make yourself look good. It is still going to be sin. Here I go again. I know, I know, the bible but, it tells us this very thing "For all have sinned and come short of the glory of god" (Roman 3:23).

It doesn't stop at gambling, adultery, drinking, drugging, or overeating. Sin can cover a lot of territories. There are a lot of stones being cast. Are we guilty before we decide to cast!

Please do not try to label the next person as the worst sinner you have ever seen. Think about all your sins you have made and buried deep in your closet and you continue to make. Again, making an impression in front of man is not your problem because he is full of sin too. You cannot hide it from God.

Past

Why do we keep living in the past? Live for the present and plan and look for the future. Some things in your past have not been the most productive things in your life. But it can be hard to let it go.

If God is in your life, then trust him and trust that he will do all things that are best for you. We can take a step or two back in our past and get stuck in a rut over and over again. What are we accomplishing?

Do not sell yourself short. If you want God to open another door, then close the door in your past. Trust and accept and appreciate the door he has opened for you. You will go far in your life.

Plan a positive future; speak negatively and you will likely get negativity. If you try speaking positively then positivity will likely come. Make a step in the positive direction, not only for you, but also for your family and surroundings.

The past is gone. Our future depends on us and what we do in the present. It is like most things. It comes one day at a time.

Confidence

Have confidence in yourself. You do not have to settle or accept less. It is easy to see someone else with a problem. But, most of the time, we cannot see or accept that we have a problem. If we see we have a problem, it is much harder to act on it for improvement.

Christ is our life. Do not be a self-defeater. Here is the bible again—"I can do all things through Christ which strengtheneth me" (Philippians 4:13).

It is the relationship with God that gives you confidence. God is the strength and power that no one or nothing should be more powerful or controlling in your life than him. I do not think God will ask or tell you to do something that he knows you are not capable of doing. Think about it; how can you fail if he's telling you to do something, and he controls you? God is not a failure.

Death

Death is so final. There is no more saying; I'm sorry to that person. Whatever words that we have spoken or whatever we have done in that person's life is something we will have to live with for the rest of our lives.

Sometimes, when we think we are doing something to hurt someone else, remember, God is watching every step and hearing every word. Please do not think you are doing something so great when you hurt the next person, and your words make you feel good.

Sometimes, it does not have to be words. "You can nitpick at someone," Momma would say. You will reap what you sow and it will be here on this earth, not after death. He can put a hurt on you, worse than the hurt you put on someone else. There is no getting around it.

Sometimes, God will take away from you more than you have ever thought you took from someone else. So please be careful! It is not your revenge or someone else's revenge you need to worry about because God said, "Vengeance is mine." Now, that is who you need to worry about, not man.

Check up

Check up on your parents and grandparents. If you cannot visit, pick up the telephone and call. It will be appreciated, even if it is not mentioned.

As mentioned earlier, time is precious. We must remember time is not always on our side. Not only will it be a good thing for the older generation, but, one day, if you do not die first, you too will be at the mercy of someone else. Keep in mind whatever you put into life will be what you will receive.

Wesley B. would say, "You will reap what you sow! And if you dig ditches for someone else, you might fall in it yourself!" You never know who might have to give you your last drink of water. Show the elderly some love, and let them know you have not forgotten them. The price of real love is no charge. Wisdom usually comes with age, but there are times when illness and old age can come alone.

In closing

Love and respect yourself and other people. If you keep God first in your life, you'll keep the peace in your heart. Set a goal and work at it. Lastly, whatever you do, *don't give up*.

Daily Reading

1. "The Lord is gracious and compassionate; slow to anger and rich in love" (Psalms 145:8).

2. "For his anger lasts only a moment, but his favor lasts a lifetime; weeping may remain for a night, but rejoicing comes in the morning" (Psalms 30:5).

3. "A quick-tempered man does foolish things . . ." (Proverbs 14:17).

4. "In your anger do not sin". Do not let the sun go down while you are still angry. (Ephesians 4:26)

5. "For God so loved the world that he gave his one and only Son, that whoever believes in him shall not perish but have eternal life" (John 3:16).

6. "Then Jesus declared, 'I am the bread of life. He who comes to me will never go hungry, and he who believes in me will never be thirsty'" (John 6:35).

7. "I tell you the truth; he who believes has everlasting life" (John 6:47).

8. "Give and it will be given to you. A good measure, pressed down, shaken together and running over, will be poured into your lap. For with the measure you use, it will be measured to you" (Luke 6:38).

9. "I was young and now I am old, yet I have never seen the righteous forsaken or their children begging bread. They are always generous and lend freely; their children will be blessed" (Psalms 37:25-26).

10. "Be careful not to do your 'acts of righteousness' before men, to be seen by them. If you do, you will have no reward from your Father in heaven. "So when you give to the needy, do not announce it with trumpets, as the hypocrites do in the synagogues and on the streets, to be honored by men. I tell you the truth; they have received their reward in full. But when you give to the needy, do not let your left hand know what your right hand is doing, so that your giving may be in secret. Then your

Father, who sees what is done in secret, will reward you."
(Matthew 6:1-4).

11. "They relied, 'Believe in the Lord Jesus, and you will be
    saved you and your household'" (Acts 16:31).
12. "The promise is for you and your children and for all
    who are far off-for all whom the Lord our God will call".
13. "Children's children are a crown to the aged, and parents
    are the pride of their children" (Proverbs 17:6).
14. "Children, obey your parents in the Lord, for this is
    right. "Honor your father and mother"—which is the
    first commandment with a promise—"that it may go well
    with you and that you may enjoy long life on the earth"
    (Ephesians 6:1-3).
15. "A wise son brings joy to his father, but a foolish son grief
    to his mother" (Proverbs 10:1).
16. "Listen to your father, who gave you, life; and do not
    despise your mother when she is old" (Proverbs 23:22).
17. "The Lord is my rock, my fortress and my deliverer; my
    God is my rock, in whom; I take refuge. He is my shield
    and the horn of my salvation, my stronghold" (Psalms
    18:2).
18. "Cast your cares on the Lord and he will sustain you; he
    will never let the righteous fall" (Psalms 55:22).
19. "Wait for the Lord; be strong and take heart and wait for
    the Lord" (Psalms 27:14).
20. "Keep your lives free from the love of money and be
    content with what you have, because God has said,
    'Never will I leave you; never will I forsake you'" (Hebrew
    13:5).
21. "A heart at peace gives life to the body, but envy rots the
    bones" (Proverbs 14:30).
22. "Trust in the Lord and do good; dwell in the land and
    enjoy safe pasture" (Psalms 37:3).
23. "Be strong and take heart, all you who hope in the Lord"
    (Psalms 31:24).

24. "Even though I walk through the shadow of death, I will fear no evil, for you are with me; your rod and your staff, they comfort me" (Psalms 23:4).
25. "The Lord is my strength and my shield; my heart trusted in Him, and I am helped; therefore my heart greatly rejoices. And with my song I will praise Him. (Psalm 28:7)
26. "When a man's ways are pleasing to the Lord, he makes even his enemies live at peace with him" (Proverbs 16:7).
27. "All who rage against you will surely be shamed and disgraced those who oppose you will be as nothing and perish. Though you search for your enemies, you will not find them. Those who wage war against you will be as nothing at all" (Isaiah 41:11-12).
28. "Peace I leave with you; my peace I give you. I do not give to you as the world gives. Do not let your hearts be troubled and do not be afraid." (John 14:27)
29. "Now faith is being sure of what we hope for and certain of what we do not see" (Hebrews 11:1).
30. "For it is by grace you have been saved, through faith—and this not from yourselves, it is the gift of God" (Ephesians 2:8).
31. "We live by faith, not by sight" (2 Corinthians 5:7).

Good Rules to Follow

- Always be honest (Proverbs 12:22).
- Count your blessing (Psalms 34:1-3).
- Bear each other's burdens (Galatians 6:2).
- Forgive and forget (Micah 7:18).
- Be kind and tender hearted (Ephesians 4:32).
- Comfort one another (1 Thessalonians 4:32).
- Keep your promise (Romans 4:21).
- Be supportive of one another (Acts 20:35).
- Be true to each other (Revelation 15:3).
- Look after each other (Deuteronomy 15:3).
- Treat each other like you treat your friends (Mathews 7:12).
- But, most importantly, love one another deeply from the heart (1 Peter 1:22).

Trust Me

I took care of you when you were a child

Even though, you were sick once in a while.

Walked you to school on your first day

And I taught you how to pray.

I was up with you during the night

I even tucked you in ever so tight.

I, Protected you from the bullies while you were in school.

Putting my arms around you even when you broke a rule

Guided you throughout your teenage years

Consoled you and wiped away your tears.

No matter what your gains were or what you had

And no matter how much you fussed and got mad.

You are grown up, with a good start

I will remain in your heart.

I will be with you in your future days

Because I am "God" I will be with you always.